Gustave Flaubert

Titles in the series Critical Lives present the work of leading cultural figures of the modern period. Each book explores the life of the artist, writer, philosopher or architect in question and relates it to their major works.

In the same series

Gustave Flaubert

Anne Green

REAKTION BOOKS

BOOK. Always too long, whatever it is.
Gustave Flaubert, *Dictionary of Received Ideas*

Published by Reaktion Books Ltd
Unit 32, Waterside
44–48 Wharf Road
London N1 7UX, UK

www.reaktionbooks.co.uk

First published 2017
Copyright © Anne Green 2017

Printed and bound in Great Britain by Bell & Bain, Glasgow

A catalogue record for this book is available from the British Library

ISBN 978 1 78023 820 3

Contents

Gustave Flaubert, photographed by Étienne Carjat.

Introduction

INTRODUCTION. Obscene word.

Gustave Flaubert, *Dictionary of Received Ideas*

Gustave Flaubert despised literary biography. He was adamant that a writer's personal life should remain private, and when he was approached about a potential biography soon after the publication of *Madame Bovary*, his response was unambiguous:

> I have no biography! . . . Life is impossible nowadays! No sooner do you become an artist, than grocers, register-checkers, customs officials, petty bootmakers and others feel the need to entertain themselves with your personal details! There are people to tell them whether you are dark or fair, mischievous or melancholic, aged such-and-such, fond of the bottle or keen on harmonica-playing. I, on the contrary, believe that a writer should leave nothing behind but his works. His life matters little.[1]

But as well as his works, Flaubert left a great deal of himself behind. He poured his turbulent emotional life into youthful, semi-autobiographical writings that were not intended for publication, and for a year or so he kept a journal of his intimate thoughts. In the notebook that always accompanied him on his extensive travels, he recorded his experiences and reactions, and he made detailed notes at key moments in his life, such as the death of a close friend or his attendance at a grand ball given by Emperor Napoléon III for Tsar Alexander II, William I of Prussia and Otto von Bismarck. To entertain George Sand, he even composed a mock biography full of recognizably autobiographical elements, *The Life and Works of Reverend Father Cruchard* (*Vie et travaux du R. P. Cruchard*). He also left more than four thousand letters, which convey a vivid picture of his everyday life, his opinions and his quirky personality.

Far from having no biography, Flaubert has had many. Even during his lifetime, writers such as the Goncourt brothers chronicled their encounters with him, and after his death, other friends, including Émile Zola, Guy de Maupassant, Maxime Du Camp and his niece Caroline, published their personal memories of the great writer. Many biographers have written about him since, attracted by his eventful life and volatile character as well as by his influential genius. No biography, however, can hope to capture fully Flaubert's defiantly original imagination or the paradoxes of his iconoclastic, sensitive, irascible, humorous, combative and loyal nature. He would certainly have agreed, for attempting to tidy ideas away into a neat conclusion was, in his view, the ultimate sign of stupidity. For the fullest sense of Gustave Flaubert, then, readers should go to his own writings and to his wonderful correspondence, which have been the main sources for this book.

1

The Early Years, 1821–40

DISSECTION. Insult to the majesty of death.
Gustave Flaubert, *Dictionary of Received Ideas*

'I was born in a hospital and I lived there for quarter of a century.'[1] This was how Gustave Flaubert described his early life in Normandy to the historian Jules Michelet many years later. The laconic tone, however, belies the complex reality of an often troubled childhood and youth, and of a series of disturbing early experiences that left a deep and lasting mark on the future writer.

When Flaubert was born in the Hôtel-Dieu hospital in Rouen at four o'clock in the morning on 12 December 1821, he arrived into a medical family that had had more than its share of sorrow. His mother, Anne-Justine Caroline Fleuriot, the only child of a country doctor from Normandy, had an unhappy upbringing. Her mother had died a few days after giving birth to her in 1793, during the most violent phase of the French Revolution, and Caroline was cared for by her father until he too died, leaving her an orphan at the age of nine. Relatives then sent her to board at a dame school in Honfleur run by two elderly ladies, but within a few years they too were dead, and another home had to be found. At this point, the girl's godmother took her under her wing and invited her to Rouen to stay at the Hôtel-Dieu, where her husband, Jean-Baptiste Laumonier, was chief surgeon. It was there, not long after her arrival in the city, that the fourteen-year-old Caroline Fleuriot met her future husband.

Rouen surgeon and anatomist Jean-Baptiste Laumonier copying a dissected cadaver to create one of the anatomical models for which he was famous. Painting by J. E. Heinsius, early 19th century.

Nine years older than Caroline, Achille-Cléophas Flaubert was the gifted son of a veterinarian from near Nogent-sur-Seine, 100 km (60 miles) southeast of Paris. At medical school in the capital he had studied under the famous surgeon Guillaume Dupuytren, repeatedly coming top of his year, and when Laumonier let it be known that he needed a new assistant to lecture on anatomy at the Hôtel-Dieu in Rouen, Dupuytren recommended his star pupil. Within a few months of Achille-Cléophas meeting the young Caroline Fleuriot, and with the full approval of the Laumoniers, it was agreed that the pair would marry once the bride was of age. In the meantime, she was sent off to boarding school to complete her education.

When she was eighteen, the couple married and moved into an apartment on the rue du Petit Salut, near Rouen Cathedral, and within a year Caroline had given birth to their first child, a son, whom they named Achille after his father. Between the births of Achille in 1813 and Gustave in 1821, there were three other babies: a daughter, christened Caroline after her mother and late grandmother, and two more boys, Émile-Cléophas and Jules-Alfred, but both little Caroline and Émile-Cléophas died before the age of two. By then, Achille-Cléophas had succeeded Laumonier as surgeon-in-chief at the Hôtel-Dieu, and the family had moved into accommodation in a wing of the hospital on rue de Lecat. So when Gustave was born there in December 1821, he arrived into a household still mourning the loss of their two young children and rightly fearful that death might also claim the sickly Jules-Alfred, who survived only until June 1822. With three of their children dying in the space of five years – a dreadful toll even by the standard of nineteenth-century infant mortality – it is hardly surprising that Madame Flaubert hovered anxiously over Gustave and over her next and final baby, a girl born in 1824 and named Caroline in memory of her dead sister. The successive losses of so many of those dearest to her affected Madame Flaubert deeply.

The wing of the Hôtel-Dieu, Rouen, in which the Flaubert family lived from 1818.

Melancholy, reserved, undemonstrative and often incapacitated by severe migraines, which she treated with laudanum, she seemed severe and cold to those who did not know her well. But her devotion to her surviving family was unconditional, and for the rest of her life she watched over her children as if death were poised to snatch them away at any moment.

Gustave, however, was a healthy baby and a robust little boy – so attractive, family legend had it, that when the Duchesse de Berry, mother of the heir presumptive to the French throne, visited Rouen and caught sight of him in his father's arms, she ordered her carriage to stop to let her admire the infant. He grew into a quiet and reflective child who liked to spend hours sitting motionless, sucking his finger, lost in thought; his family wondered if he might be slow-witted. But life in and around the hospital provided much for the little boy to ponder on: pale, sick patients; bodies on stretchers;

his father's medical books, with their graphic images of deformed and diseased limbs; and the macabre anatomical teaching models, with their exposed blood vessels, internal organs and staring eyeballs made of brightly coloured wax, for which Laumonier had become famous. There were also frightening encounters with insane, semi-naked inmates, who howled and clawed at their faces as they tried to free themselves from their restraints. And there were the disturbing sights that Flaubert and his little sister witnessed when they climbed the garden trellis and peered down through the vine leaves into the hospital mortuary. Through its open windows they would watch their father dissecting cadavers, until he noticed the children and chased them away. Flaubert never forgot the fat flies that buzzed back and forth between the corpses and the vines; the strangely sinister buzzing insects that appear in many of his novels may well have originated in that mortuary. But the hospital was not the only source of troubling scenes. Another from around the same time – when Flaubert was six or seven years old – was one glimpsed as he crossed the old market square in Rouen, where Joan of Arc had been burned at the stake four centuries earlier. As he passed, he saw fresh blood glistening on the cobblestones and looked up to see men unhooking the basket of a guillotine that had just done its work. He already knew about guillotines, for he had often heard how his own paternal grandfather had been imprisoned and condemned to death during the Reign of Terror, and been saved from execution only by the timely fall of Robespierre.

All these scenes were absorbed by the impressionable little boy. They lodged in his mind, mingling with violent images of blood and fire from the terrifying tales of E.T.A. Hoffmann ('I felt and *saw* everything in . . . Hoffmann,' Flaubert would later recall) and with elements of the uncanny from the folktales of which Julie Hébert, a young country girl hired as a household help, was an inexhaustible source.[2] (Julie – the Flauberts changed her name from Caroline to avoid confusion when she entered their service in 1825 – would

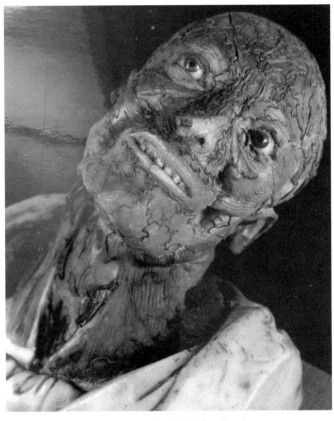

Nineteenth-century French anatomical model of a flayed head.

remain with the family for nearly sixty years, a much-loved presence in their lives.) Blood-stained images seeped into the young Flaubert's dreams. Colouring the pictures in a children's book, he made everything, including the sea, red. His sleep was disturbed by blood-filled nightmares in which men with half-flayed faces threatened him with gleaming knives. Even his understanding of language was shaped by these images, so that when he said he wanted to 'give his heart' to a little girl, in his mind's eye he saw a real human heart nestling among oysters in a straw-lined basket. Although in later life he would talk with amused detachment about these childish terrors, they had embedded themselves in his memory forever. However hard he might try to suppress them, they were never far below the surface, constantly threatening to push themselves to the fore.

But there were happier times, too, for the young boy. An annual highlight was the fair of Saint-Romain, which took place in Rouen every autumn. The Flaubert children joined townspeople and peasants from the surrounding area who flocked to its carnival atmosphere, excitingly at odds with the town's normally staid formality. There were brightly painted sideshows, coloured lights, lively music, displays of freaks and wild animals, and – particularly entrancing to Flaubert – Père Legrain's puppet theatre, whose wooden saint, pig and devil marionettes acted out, year after year, the Temptation of St Anthony. Flaubert also enjoyed visiting a kind-hearted elderly neighbour, Monsieur Mignot, who liked the boy and entertained him with an endless fund of stories. Mignot's grandson, Ernest Chevalier, often came to stay. Eighteen months older than Flaubert, and sharing his grandfather's love of literature, Ernest soon became a bosom friend to Flaubert. It was Mignot who introduced the boys to the adventures of Don Quixote and Sancho Panza. Flaubert adored Cervantes's novel, with its fusion of reality and illusion, and would later claim that all his own work had its origins in that book, which dominated his imagination even before he could read.

With willing storytellers like Julie and Mignot around, Flaubert showed no interest in learning to read for himself. He preferred to listen, watch and think, and when his mother tried to teach him the alphabet, she found him an unreceptive pupil. He did not learn to read properly until he was about eight years old, long after his little sister had acquired the skill. Almost as soon as he could read, however, Flaubert wanted to write. One of his earliest surviving letters, written just after his ninth birthday

Gustave Flaubert aged about eight, drawn by his brother Achille.

and sprinkled with spelling mistakes, urges Ernest to come and stay in the Hôtel-Dieu so that they can write together: 'I would write plays and you can write down your dreams,' he pleads.[3]

Devising plays to perform with Caroline and friends quickly became an overwhelming passion for Flaubert. When he looked back at this period from the only slightly self-mocking perspective of a seventeen-year-old, he remembered the intensity of his childhood ambition:

When I was ten, I was already dreaming of glory, and I started composing as soon as I learned to write. I conjured up delightful pictures for myself: I dreamed of a theatre full of light and gold, with applauding hands, shouts of praise and bouquets of flowers. People are calling 'Author! Author!'; the author really is me, it is my name, me, me! They search for me in the corridors, in the dressing rooms; they crane forward to catch a glimpse of me, the curtain rises, I step forward: what bliss! They look at you, they admire you, they envy you, they are proud to love you and to have seen you![4]

In reality, however, Flaubert's theatrical performances took place at home, in the family's billiard room before a small audience of family, servants and possibly the occasional medical student. He organized posters, tickets, costumes and backdrop, and the billiard table, pushed to one end of the room, served as a makeshift stage for his dramatic experiments. By March 1832 he had accumulated nearly thirty of these, including an irreverent farce entitled *Preparations for Receiving the King* (*Les Apprêts pour recevoir le roi*), inspired by a visit to Rouen the previous year by the new monarch, Louis-Philippe. Acting in the plays he created – inhabiting characters and situations of his own imagining – seems to have satisfied a deep need in the boy. His acute powers of observation made him an excellent mimic, and he took great delight in performing before his captive audience. So intense were his attempts to get inside the skin of people who caught his attention that his father feared he would cause himself harm and ordered him, unsuccessfully, to stop. Flaubert's love of acting lasted for many years, and he believed that with proper training, he could have become a great actor. True or not, his powerful urge to observe and impersonate lies at the heart of his subsequent ability to create unusually plausible fictional characters.

Meanwhile, he carried on scribbling. He was proud to show the results to his family circle, who encouraged, or at least indulged, these first literary attempts. Mignot complimented him on pieces he wrote about *Don Quixote*, and Ernest's uncle Amédée found his compositions sufficently amusing to arrange, soon after Flaubert's tenth birthday, for two of them to be privately printed under the title *Three Pages from a Schoolboy's Exercise Book, or, The Selected Works of Gustave F**** (*Trois pages d'un cahier d'écolier, ou, oeuvres choisies de Gustave F****, 1832). The pieces constituted of a eulogy to another native of Rouen, the great seventeenth-century dramatist Pierre Corneille, and a parody of a medical textbook's definition

Drawing of Gustave Flaubert by E.-H. Langlois, 1830. Langlois taught at the École des Beaux Arts in Rouen and was a friend of the Flaubert family.

of constipation – an incongrous pairing of literary veneration with gleeful iconoclasm that was to remain typical of the adult Flaubert.

As a child, however, Flaubert was desperate for companions of his own age. Like many middle-class boys of the period, he was educated at home until the age of ten, and although Caroline was a delightful and enthusiastic playmate, her company was not enough. His brother Achille was eight years older and away at school most of the time, and his earnest, studious disposition was not best suited to Flaubert's more exuberant and imaginative temperament. Flaubert's affectionate letters to Ernest are full of pleas for him to visit. In April 1832, entreating his friend to come and take part in his theatricals, Flaubert assured him, 'we are united by a kind of fraternal love . . . if necessary I would travel a thousand leagues to be with my best of friends.'[5] But this was during France's great cholera epidemic, which killed thousands in Paris amid wild rumours of mass poisoning, and claimed 75 victims in Rouen within two weeks of reaching the city. Cholera sufferers were brought to the Hôtel-Dieu, where only a simple partition with a door separated the Flaubert family's dining room from a hospital ward in which 'people were dying like flies'.[6] Small wonder that Ernest's parents were reluctant to let him visit his friend, despite Flaubert's insistence that few cholera patients remained in the hospital. For Flaubert, however, proximity to disease and death was part of normal life.

In May 1832, with the Rouen cholera epidemic at its peak, Flaubert enrolled as a day-boy at the city's Collège Royal, where Ernest was already a boarder. In his blue uniform, he arrived – like Charles Bovary – as an awkward newcomer into a class of boys who had already been together since the previous October; after the summer break, he returned as a weekly boarder. The school insisted on strict discipline, particularly after a scandalous episode the previous year when pupils had mutinied and barricaded themselves into their dormitories until forced out by water hoses. School punishments included being forced to kneel on a sharp

Flaubert's sister Caroline, aged about seven, by E.-H. Langlois.

ruler, to hold two heavy Greek dictionaries above the head, or to copy out endless Latin aphorisms. More serious miscreants were locked in the school's detention cell. The contrast between this regime and congenial home tuition with free access to his father's extensive library must have come as an unwelcome shock to Flaubert, and although he seems never to have been subjected to the cell, he was far from a model pupil. He later claimed to have won a prize for a 25-page essay on the history of the mushroom by copying most of it from a botanical reference book. His school reports mention stubborn disobedience and lack of application, and he ranked in the lower half of his year in most subjects. But despite the irksome rules and regulations, the sarcasm of teachers, the casual, mocking cruelty of other boys and the bitter cold of the dormitories – so cold that oil in the lamps would freeze overnight – Flaubert's memories of school were not all negative.

In particular, he welcomed the companionship of a small group of like-minded boys who shared his passion for literature as well as his taste for scatological humour and general irreverence. Ernest was one of them, and another was Alfred Le Poittevin, a boy whose family already had close ties with Flaubert's. Alfred's witty, light-hearted mother had attended the same little school in Honfleur as Flaubert's mother, and the two had remained friends after marriage; Achille-Cléophas became godfather to Alfred, Alfred's father was godfather to Flaubert, and Alfred's younger sister Laure (better known today as mother of the novelist Guy de Maupassant) was a much-loved companion of the Flaubert children. Although five years older than Flaubert, Alfred became one of his closest and most cherished friends; years after Alfred's death, Flaubert would remember him as the man he had loved most in the whole world and the only person who had ever really understood him.

Looking back many years later on his time at the Collège Royal, Flaubert described this group of adolescent boys, no doubt with some Romantic exaggeration, as 'a literary coterie that seethed and flared . . . with the most furiously poetic and sentimental exultation imaginable. We used to sleep with daggersunder our pillows . . . We were as beautiful as angels.'[7] Allowed little freedom by the school's strict regime, they escaped into imaginations fired by the drama and passion of the novels they strained their eyes to read in the dormitory after lights-out. Victor Hugo was their hero. Flaubert remembered the period as a strange one of intense emotional turmoil, but for some of the boys it all became too much. If Flaubert's account is to be believed, one hanged himself with his tie and another, in despair over a girl, shot himself in the head as the group 'veered between madness and suicide'.[8]

School holidays brought Flaubert escape from that highly charged atmosphere. There were family visits to Paris, with excursions to Fontainebleau, Versailles and the theatre, and family holidays in Trouville, a small seaside resort on the Normandy coast that would come to occupy a place of deep and lasting emotional significance in Flaubert's inner life. During a holiday there when he was twelve, however, he was exposed to yet another of the disturbing events that dogged his early years. A pretty young woman whom he had seen laughing with her husband the previous evening was swept out to sea and drowned while swimming with friends; would-be rescuers fished her body from the water in a net. In the nightmares that plagued Flaubert after the accident, it was his own mother who sank beneath the waves as he looked on helplessly.

Two years later, in the summer of 1836, Trouville was the backdrop to a very different experience that touched him even more profoundly. Walking along the beach one morning, he noticed the incoming tide begin to lap at the fringes of a red and black shawl that a bather had left lying on the sand, and he moved it away from the water. In the hotel restaurant that lunchtime, a young woman sitting at the next table leaned over to thank him. Her voice and her dark, voluptuous beauty transfixed the fourteen-year-old, and when he next saw her, breastfeeding her baby daughter on the beach, he felt 'as if Venus had come to life and stepped down from her pedestal'.[9] This sudden and intense adolescent infatuation with Élisa Schlésinger, the wife of an enterprising music publisher, became a memory that he treasured, nurtured and eventually transformed into Frédéric Moreau's soulful longing for Madame Arnoux in *Sentimental Education* (*L'Éducation sentimentale*, 1869). Flaubert maintained contact with the Schlésingers, and although he barely recognized her when they met a few years later, thoughts of Élisa

Lithograph of Élisa Schlésinger and her daughter by Achille Devéria, *c.* 1838.

sustained him throughout the remainder of his school days. He would later claim that she had been his only true passion.

Flaubert's school put particular emphasis on the Classics and on rhetoric, but it was in history that he excelled. As history master he was fortunate to have Adolphe Chéruel, a distinguished former pupil of Jules Michelet. Chéruel taught Flaubert at the school but also saw him for weekly private lessons, and the period spent under his tuition was crucial in stimulating the boy's interest in the past and in starting to form his critical faculties. Chéruel inculcated into all his pupils the need for precision and the fearless pursuit of truth, and the methodology that Flaubert absorbed from him coloured more than his school exercises. At the same time, however, Flaubert's interest in history was being further stimulated through visits to the theatre. Rouen offered many opportunities to see historical dramas, much in vogue in the 1830s, by writers such as Alexandre Dumas, Victor Hugo and Casimir Delavigne. Yet even when enthralled by events on stage, Flaubert was at the mercy of macabre imaginings: whenever he went to the theatre, the boy had the vivid sensation of sitting in an audience of skeletons.

Although his teachers considered that Flaubert lacked application in schoolwork other than history, his mind was far from inactive. Indeed, in his early teenage years he was almost constantly writing, entertaining himself with an outpouring of short compositions ranging from historical narratives and Gothic tales of passion and despair to a 'literary journal' complete with theatrical news. These very early pieces were sometimes clumsy and derivative, and none of them has much literary merit, but they show that Flaubert not only had a compulsion to write, but that he was already acquiring an awareness of structure, suspense and plot development, as well as a distinct taste for irony.

In April 1836, when he was fourteen, he embarked on a longer and more ambitious project, *A Perfume to Sense* (*Un parfum à sentir*), which he shaped into chapters. Challenging readers to make up their own minds, he defiantly subtitled the work as a 'philosophical, moral, immoral tale (*ad libitum*)' – an early instance of what later became a characteristic refusal to comply with convention or dictate how the reader should respond to his work. The final chapter of *A Perfume to Sense* features a graphic description of the body of a drowned woman lying on a mortuary slab. In his account of her swollen, discoloured flesh, the nauseating smell of the cadaver, the buzzing flies clustering round her mouth and the presence of medical students, one can clearly see Flaubert not only starting to transform his traumatic memories into fiction, but self-consciously revelling in that process as he comes to sense the exhilarating power of words and the relation between a writer and his public. As he tells the reader at the end,

Perhaps you do not know what a pleasure writing is!
To write, oh to write is to seize hold of the world and
its prejudices and virtues, and to sum it up in a book.
It is to feel one's thought germinate, grow, live and
rear up on its pedestal to remain there forever.[10]

Meanwhile, the precocious schoolboy continued to read insatiably – Rabelais, Montaigne, Shakespeare, Goethe, Rousseau and Byron were among his favourites – and to write. His *Memoirs of a Madman* (*Les Mémoires d'un fou*), combining autobiographical detail with intense Romantic introspection, passion, cynicism and despair, were composed in 1838, and show that he was already aware, at the age of sixteen, of the pleasure of reliving and reshaping old memories to create a new form. 'These memories were a passion,' says the narrator, while bemoaning the inadequacy of language to express his emotions.[11] Flaubert's school reports assumed that he would follow his father and his brother Achille into a career in medicine, but his interest and energies clearly lay elsewhere.

Gustave (right) and Achille Flaubert. Drawing by Delaunay, *c.* 1835.

Unlike Achille, who had recently married a conventional middle-class woman whom Flaubert never grew to like, he kicked against conformity. While his grades improved markedly in his final year of school, his reluctance to follow apparently senseless rules and regulations never waned, and he and his friends grew increasingly exasperated by the staff's petty-minded authoritarianism. (Flaubert could not contain his glee when a staff member whom he particularly resented was sacked after being caught, as he put it in a jubilant letter to Ernest Chevalier, 'brothelizing in a brothel'.[12]) Matters came to a head towards the end of the first term, when his philosophy class refused to comply with a thousand-line punishment for noisy behaviour. Despite their protests to the headmaster, students who still refused to cooperate were threatened with expulsion. Flaubert stood his ground, and in December 1839, a few days after his eighteenth birthday, he was duly expelled along with four others from what he furiously called 'that bloody bedlam of shit of a school'.[13] But if he was to go to university, as the career plan that had been mapped out for him assumed he would, he needed to pass his baccalaureate exams that summer. Independent study at home was the only option. He confided to his journal that despite a few moments of buffoonery, his school days had been unimaginably boring and sad; desperate to 'tell his own story to himself', he intended to write about them one day.[14] As the exams approached, however, he threw himself feverishly into study, rising at three in the morning and spending all day at his desk, smoking his pipe, learning long sections of Demosthenes and the *Iliad* by heart, and forcing himself to cram mathematics and physics when he would have much preferred to be reading the works of the Marquis de Sade. To his parents' relief, the exams were passed, and as a reward his father arranged for him to broaden his horizons by travel. At the same age, and before embarking on his medical studies, Achille had toured Scotland with an older family friend. It was therefore decided that later in the summer, the same friend, Dr Jules Cloquet, would accompany Flaubert on a tour of the Pyrenees and Corsica.

2

Coming of Age, 1840–44

LITERATURE. Pastime of the idle.

Gustave Flaubert, *Dictionary of Received Ideas*

By eighteen, Flaubert had grown into a tall, handsome, broad-shouldered youth with a resonant voice, expansive gestures and a loud, explosive laugh. The passport issued to him on 12 August 1840 for his journey to the south records his official description: 1.82 m (nearly 6 ft) tall, fair complexion, light brown hair, grey eyes, small mouth, oval face, rounded chin and forehead, and a small scar above the nose.

Although excited by the prospect of travel and the freedom it would bring, Flaubert was apprehensive lest Dr Cloquet prove too restrictive a chaperone, and his heart sank when he realized that they were also to be accompanied on the journey by Dr Cloquet's unmarried sister and a priest. The group set off by coach from Paris in late August 1840, pursued by anxious letters from Madame Flaubert, who worried about accidents and illnesses that might befall her son. Throughout the journey Flaubert made notes of his impressions, a practice he later followed whenever he travelled. The first stage south through Blois and Tours to Bordeaux he found uninspiring. Bordeaux itself seemed as dully bourgeois as Rouen, but with a more sluggish river. He would have preferred to bypass the kind of attractions that his companions' guidebooks recommended, for all the sites

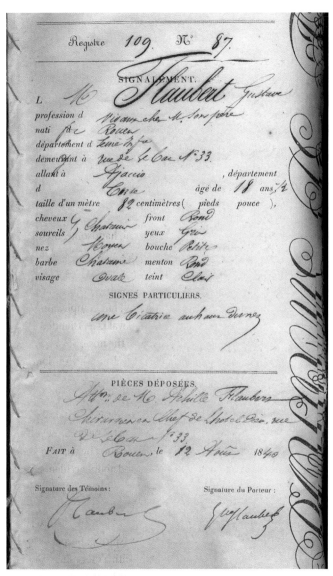

The passport issued to Flaubert on 12 August 1840 for his journey to the Pyrenees and Corsica.

described as 'interesting' or 'most curious' seemed deeply boring to him, and it was with some reluctance that he endured a lengthy guided tour of a porcelain factory. More to his taste was a visit to the catacombs beneath the basilica of St Michael, where the hollow eyes of the mummified bodies arranged in circular stacks seemed to stare back at him, but he was glad to leave Bordeaux.

As the party continued south towards Bayonne and Biarritz and saw the Pyrenees rise up before them, Flaubert's spirits began to lift, but a chilling incident in Biarritz put paid to his growing elation. While walking along the almost deserted beach, he heard shouts of distress and realized that two men were drowning offshore. A strong swimmer, Flaubert stripped off his clothes and plunged into the sea, but he was eventually forced to return to the beach without having been able to save the men or retrieve a body. Describing the drownings in his journal, he included neither sympathy for the victims nor his own feelings of distress. Instead, in what would become a characteristic move, he suppressed his emotions and transformed the tragedy into a farcical mishap that culminated in the difficulty in relocating his clothes and the discomfort of wearing wet trousers: 'For me, that was the most tragic aspect of the adventure.'[1]

After Biarritz, the group continued across the Pyrenees, dipping briefly into Spain and stopping to sightsee at 'places of interest'. More interesting to Flaubert, however, were inconsequential, idiosyncratic details: a hotel visitors' book filled with hyperbolic praise of the local trout, or a travelling salesman's lecture on the advantages of living in Spain. One evening, Flaubert treated Dr Cloquet and his sister to a reading of his travel notes. Used to reading his work aloud to his appreciative family, he expected compliments, but the Cloquets were bemused and unimpressed by their companion's unconventional travelogue, and Flaubert found himself having to fight back tears of disappointment.

His mood was probably worsened by the fact that the luggage he had sent on ahead had still not reached him, and his only pair of trousers – a thick, winter pair – were uncomfortable in the baking heat. When they reached the ancient Roman sites in Provence, however, all Flaubert's misgivings about the trip fell away. Visiting the Pont du Gard aqueduct and the Roman arenas in Nîmes and Arles was a revelation. He and his companions arrived at the Nîmes arena as the sun was setting, and in the dying light, the deserted amphitheatre seemed to conjure visions of gladiatorial combats, baying crowds and blood-soaked sand. The ancient world that Flaubert knew only from books came vividly to life for him, and although the partially excavated Roman monuments reminded him of skeletons lying half-buried in shallow graves, for the next two days he was delighted to be able to 'live in the midst of Antiquity'.[2]

In Marseilles, Flaubert and Dr Cloquet said goodbye to their companions and set off for Corsica. After a stormy sixteen-hour crossing during which Flaubert was desperately seasick – a condition described in epic detail in his journal – they reached Ajaccio on 5 October. If Flaubert's reaction to Nîmes and Arles had been mediated and intensified by his studies of classical Rome, his response to Corsica was equally shaped by his reading, particularly by Romantic writers' taste for wild and desolate landscapes and by the tales of banditry he had enjoyed as a young boy. Corsica felt gloriously untamed and ancient, and the physiognomy of its inhabitants reminded him of profiles stamped on Roman coins. There was, however, one modern tourist site that he was happy to visit: the house in Ajaccio where Napoléon Bonaparte had been born just over seventy years earlier. With a combination of awe and derision, Flaubert noted not only the metal banisters on which the future Emperor's hand had once rested and the green-spotted wallpaper of his bedroom, but the fact that next to the bed lay a farming manual about fertilizers.

For the most part, Flaubert's Corsican experience took place off the beaten track, as he and Dr Cloquet travelled for days on horseback and on foot across the island's rugged interior, accompanied by a guide and two armed infantrymen. At one point, a shot rang out ahead and the group advanced in trepidation, but the bandits they feared turned out only to be hunters. Above all, Flaubert was entranced by the landscape. With its intense colours, precipitous mountain tracks and hot, resinous scents rising from the *maquis*, Corsica must have seemed the very antithesis of Normandy. He tried to capture the unfamiliar effects in words: the changing light on mountain peaks; the thin, blue vapour that floated above steep gorges; the circular ripples made by dolphins playing in the Mediterranean far below; and the singing of distant shepherds. The whole experience felt far removed not only from France, but from the nineteenth century – it was as if he had stepped back into a past that he already knew from books. Eager to disorient himself even further, he imagined a Corsica of the future, full of restaurants and traffic.

Eventually, it was time to return to the mainland. After a calm crossing, the pair arrived back in Toulon on 19 October and made their way to Marseilles, returning to the hotel in rue de la Darse where they had stayed with their companions three weeks before. The cold, wet weather already felt autumnal, but Flaubert's adventure was not quite over. At the hotel, the proprietress's daughter, Eulalie Foucaud, a married woman in her mid-thirties, took a fancy to the youth. She enticed Flaubert to her room and they spent a memorably erotic night together. The following day, Flaubert and Dr Cloquet set out on the long journey back to Rouen, but memories of that night lingered on. Over the next six months, Eulalie sent Flaubert a series of passionate love letters, almost certainly copied from a book, and he replied in an equally passionate vein. Later, he would say that he had had no tender feelings for her other than those conjured up by the act of writing – that his love letters to Eulalie were merely a form of literary exercise. This, however, was the version of events he gave a jealous mistress and is unlikely to have been the whole truth, for in years to come he made a point of seeking out the hotel whenever he visited Marseilles, though it was always closed. Passing by eighteen years later, he found the building transformed into a bazaar with a barber's shop on the first floor, which he twice visited to have his beard shaved. Returning there moved him deeply in ways he could not quite explain.

In October 1840, however, it was a matter of travelling back north to Rouen and rain and leafless trees. Flaubert was not pleased to be home. He hated Normandy, France and Europe, he told Ernest Chevalier, and dreamed of escaping again to the hot south, to Spain, Italy, Greece, Turkey or Egypt, or to the great cities of antiquity – Babylon, Nineveh, Persepolis or Palmyra. 'I wanted to leave home – leave myself; go anywhere at all,' he later explained.[3] But leaving himself was easier said than done, and although thoughts of a medical career had long been abandoned, and he had resigned himself to having to study law in Paris eventually, he had no real plans for the future. For reasons that are unclear – health, perhaps – he did not go to university that autumn, but instead spent the year at home, disconsolate. His journal from the period is filled with philosophical musings on life and love, but above all, it shows his overwhelming preoccupation with writing and his acute awareness of the difficulty of capturing the truth. Ten contradictory thoughts could pass through his mind during the composition of a single sentence. 'When I started this', he wrote,

I wanted it to be a faithful copy of what I was thinking and feeling, and not once has that happened, so much does a man lie to himself. You look at yourself in the mirror but your image is reversed. In short, it is impossible to tell the truth when you write.[4]

Nonetheless, he finished the written account of his travels and immediately embarked on the longest piece he had so far attempted, a novella entitled *November* (*Novembre*). A partly autobiographical tale of adolescent longing, passion and despair, this first-person narrative follows its world-weary young hero through extremes of emotion which crystallize around the voluptuous figure of Marie, a prostitute with whom he spends one long and passionate night and who is clearly modelled on Eulalie Foucaud. But translating his imaginative fervour onto the page seemed almost impossible. Bogged down in self-doubt, perhaps depressed, perhaps unwell, he found himself increasingly incapable of doing anything at all. Days passed without him opening a book, and in his lethargic state he was putting on weight; 'I'm becoming colossal, vast, I'm an ox, a sphinx, a bittern, an elephant, a whale, whatever is hugest, fattest and heaviest, in mind as well as body,' he told Ernest the following July.[5] Even the family's annual summer holiday in Trouville failed to raise his spirits, though he arrived bearing volumes of Virgil, Shakespeare and Homer, 'three masters who alone are worth all the libraries in the world, three oceans, three worlds of poetry and ideas.'[6] Writing seemed beyond him. All he could do was eat, drink, sleep and smoke: as he reported to Ernest, 'I'm bored, bored, bored . . . I'm stupid, idiotic and inert.'[7]

In November 1841, shortly before his twentieth birthday, Flaubert finally enrolled at the Faculty of Law in Paris. He was the most reluctant of students. After two months he had still not opened a law book, hoping to scrape through by cramming for fifteen hours a day before the exams, which if necessary could be postponed until July or even December. Instead, he continued to read in Greek and Latin, and to write. With *November* nearly finished, he felt he had arrived at a critical point in his life: the prospect of becoming a lawyer filled him with horror, for all that mattered to him was literature, but he needed to know whether he had any real talent for writing. Would his novella, with its psychological analyses and lack of plot, be any good, or was it, as he feared, 'very false, and quite pretentious and stilted'?[8] Family expectations pushed him in the direction of law, which was also the path taken by Ernest Chevalier and Alfred Le Poittevin, but writing was his 'old love', his obsession.[9]

And so the year passed with very little study of the law, although Flaubert did stay on in Paris instead of spending the whole summer in Trouville with his family as usual. After a desperate attempt to borrow classmates' notes to submit as evidence that he had attended lectures and was therefore eligible to sit the July examinations, he abandoned the plan and postponed the exams until December. In mid-August, then, he could finally join his family at the seaside, where his Trouville regime was pleasantly undemanding:

> I get up at eight, have breakfast, smoke, swim, eat again, smoke, sunbathe, have dinner, smoke again and go to bed again in order to dine again, smoke again and have lunch again . . . I read Ronsard, Rabelais and Horace, but I do it little and rarely, like eating truffles.[10]

There were agreeable social encounters, too – particularly with the Colliers, an expatriate English family with two daughters, Gertrude and her invalid sister Henrietta, whom Caroline had befriended earlier that summer. One evening, the friendship was sealed in dramatic fashion when muslin curtains in the Colliers' house blew against a candle and caught fire. Seeing the flames from his window, Flaubert rushed to rescue the bedridden Henrietta and carry her downstairs to safety before transferring her to his family's house for the night, for Dr Flaubert worried that the shock might aggravate the delicate girl's condition. Both sisters were greatly taken with the handsome young Flaubert, who in turn was pleased to find intelligent companions eager to discuss literature. Years later, Gertrude remembered him as having 'the great charm of the utter unconsciousness of his own physical and mental beauty', and the ideas he had expressed as they sat together on the beach at Trouville, reading aloud and discussing poetry, remained fixed in her mind:

> Style for him was everything – and *la forme* was of supreme importance, and never to be lost sight of . . . All ideas however grand – were nothing without style. And no thought could be beautiful unless beautifully expressed.[11]

Back in Paris after the summer, Flaubert socialized, visited brothels, exchanged affectionate and humorous letters with Caroline, and again did little studying. He saw many friends – among them the Collier sisters, Dr Cloquet and the Schlésingers – and he continued to write. In October 1842 he completed *November*, and that December, somewhat to his surprise, he finally passed his first law examinations.

With the immediate pressure of exams removed, Flaubert resumed his former habits. Although he claimed to be attending law school, he rarely set foot in the place and reported to Ernest that he was 'doing literature and art all hours of the day and night'.[12] In February 1843 he embarked on a new literary venture, more ambitious than anything he had attempted so far: this time, he planned a full-scale novel with a contemporary setting entitled *Sentimental Education*, a name he would famously reuse a quarter of a century later. Unlike *Memoirs of a Madman* and *November*, the first *Sentimental Education* is not overtly autobiographical, yet it reveals much about Flaubert's personal and artistic development at the time. The self-examination that dominated the earlier works is here split between the characters of Jules and Henry, close friends since their school days. This device of having as central characters two male friends who act as foils for one another was one to which Flaubert would return in later novels: the intriguing relationships between Mâtho and Spendius in *Salammbô* (1862), between Frédéric and Deslauriers in *Sentimental Education* of

1869, and between the eponymous Bouvard and Pécuchet in his last major work, all owe something to Jules and Henry, who in turn bear the trace of Flaubert's own inner tensions. It is not hard to recognize the inspiration for Henry, who at the start of the novel is an eighteen-year-old coming to Paris to study law, but who neglects his studies for an ultimately disillusioning love affair with his landlord's wife – or indeed the inspiration for Jules, an aspiring young writer, melancholy and introspective, who dreams of poetry, art and antiquity. Although at school the friends share the same dreams and ambitions, once in contact with the outside world their paths gradually diverge, with Jules immersing himself in the Romantic writings of Chateaubriand, Goethe and Byron, and Henry coming to prefer newspapers to poetry. Torn as he was between dutifully following a career in law and pursuing his *idée fixe* of writing, Flaubert projected his dilemma onto Jules and Henry, yet his ironic portrayal of the two friends was bitterly self-mocking. As both characters gradually abandon their youthful illusions, Jules' pretensions as a writer are mercilessly ridiculed, as is the brash success of Henry, who by the end of the novel is a wealthy bourgeois, a ruthless member of the establishment. If Flaubert was confronting his own inner conflicts in this uneven work, he did not spare the self-criticism.

There were many interruptions to the writing of the first *Sentimental Education*, including periods when Flaubert worked so intensely to catch up on his law studies that his limbs twitched and his hands shook. But there were also social distractions. One of the new friends he had made in Paris was Maxime Du Camp, the son of a wealthy surgeon, with whom he would develop a long and sometimes prickly relationship. Du Camp's memoirs contain a vivid description of his impressions of Flaubert at this time:

> His strong constitution enabled him to withstand fatigue;
> he could spend nights working on his law, which he did not

understand at all, then run around all day, dine in town, go to a show, and still remain perfectly alert and full of his natural gravity, mixing pleasure with study, spending money like water, complaining of poverty, spending fifty francs on his dinner one day and living off a crust of bread and a piece of chocolate the next, chanting prose, bellowing verse, becoming obsessed with a particular word which he would repeat ad nauseam, filling everywhere with his noise, dismissive of women who were attracted by his good looks, coming to wake me at three in the morning to go and look at moonlight on the Seine, despairing at being unable to find decent Pont-l'Évêque cheese in Paris, inventing sauces to accompany brill, and wanting to punch Gustave Planche for defaming Victor Hugo.[13]

Flaubert, Du Camp and other friends, including Alfred Le Poittevin, often met for dinner and conversation. Their favourite haunt was Dagneau's restaurant in the rue de l'Ancienne-Comédie, where they regularly talked and argued until closing time. What did they talk about? Everything except politics, according to Du Camp – anything from philosophical abstractions such as the nature of God or the identity of the self, to the latest satirical article or popular farce. Flaubert frequently gave voice impressions of actors he had seen, once infuriating his companions by continuing to talk in the distinctive drawl of the famous actress Marie Dorval for weeks on end.

Du Camp does not record whether Flaubert discussed the letters that arrived regularly from home. Those from Caroline were delightful – affectionate, teasing and full of amusing snippets of news, details of their father's latest property deals and entertaining gossip about the family's wide circle of friends, one of whom, Flaubert's former classmate Émile Hamard, seemed to visit her rather often. What is certain, however, is that Flaubert did not discuss with Du Camp the fact that he was spending much of his

Eugène Quesnet, *Maxime Du Camp*, c. 1844.

time writing a novel. Nor, knowing that he was expected to be concentrating on his studies, did he mention it in his letters home, and with his second exam looming, he reluctantly exchanged the manuscript of *Sentimental Education* for his law books in a desperate attempt to make up for lost time. Recurrent bouts of toothache made it impossible to concentrate, however. Although the dentist could find nothing wrong with his teeth, his entire jaw was in agony, the pain prevented him from sleeping and he felt exhausted. As he had feared, he failed his examination in August.

His family had arrived in Paris on the day of the exam after a three-day journey by coach from Rouen. To Caroline's disappointment, Flaubert had dissuaded them from taking the new Paris–Rouen railway, which had opened with much fanfare that May and which would have reduced the journey to four hours. How his parents reacted to the news of Flaubert's result is unknown, but his ambitious father is unlikely to have been pleased, particularly since Flaubert had overspent his allowance and pleaded for extra cash during the course of the term.

Whatever their initial response, Flaubert rejoined his family for the summer and by September had quietly resumed work on *Sentimental Education*. Although he eventually began law revision again, his mind was poorly focused on study, for in Paris that autumn he discovered more interesting social circles. In particular, he started to frequent the studio of James Pradier, one of the foremost sculptors of the day. Pradier had made a small statuette of Dr Flaubert in 1834, the year that his erotic marble sculpture of *Satyr and Bacchante* – rumoured to be based on Pradier himself and his then mistress, the actress Juliette Drouet – had scandalized visitors to the Paris Salon. By 1843, however, Pradier had completed many major public commissions and was married to Louise d'Arcet, the sister of one of Flaubert's classmates. His studio and his wife's lively presence attracted a stimulating mix of friends, including musicians, writers and politicians, and Flaubert loved going there. It made him feel at ease. As he told his sister, it was 'absolutely [his] sort of place'.[14]

It was in Pradier's studio, in November 1843, that Flaubert met his great hero, Victor Hugo. Describing the encounter to Caroline afterwards, he tried to sound blasé but soon gave in to outright adulation:

You are waiting for details about V. Hugo. What do you want me to say? He's a man who looks much like any other, with a fairly ugly face and a fairly ordinary exterior. He has magnificent teeth, a superb forehead, and no eyelashes or eyebrows. He says little, he seems to be watching himself and unwilling to give anything away. He is very polite and rather stiff. I very much like the sound of his voice. I enjoyed gazing at him from close to; I looked at him in wonderment as if he were a chest full of treasure and regal diamonds, and I reflected on everything produced by this man sitting right next to me on a little chair, and I stared at his right hand which has written so many beautiful things. This was the man who made my heart beat the fastest ever, and of all the people I am not acquainted with, he is perhaps the one I most love . . . The great man and I talked the most; I can't remember whether what I said was good or stupid.[15]

To find himself, aged 21, engaged in a serious discussion 'about torture, vengeance, thieves, etc.' with France's most celebrated living writer doubtless made the prospect of becoming a lawyer seem less attractive than ever to Flaubert.[16] After dinner one evening, he decided to confide his literary ambitions to Maxime Du Camp, knowing that he, too, wanted to become a writer. As Du Camp recalled the scene many years later, Flaubert swore his friend to secrecy before removing the manuscript of *November* from a locked chest and reading the entire work aloud to him. Dawn was breaking by the time he finished, and Du Camp's enthusiastic reaction and the ensuing exchange of artistic theories and shared ambitions brought the two young friends even closer.

When apart, they corresponded almost daily. But suddenly, without explanation, Flaubert's letters stopped. Eventually, Du Camp received a letter from Madame Flaubert inviting him to visit his friend in Rouen and explaining that an injured hand prevented Flaubert from writing. In the family apartment in the

Hôtel-Dieu, Du Camp found Flaubert in pain, his arm in a sling, and with his family keeping constant watch over him. The full story that emerged concerned much more than an injured hand, however, and it would change the course of Flaubert's life.

Returning from Deauville with his brother in their cabriolet one night at the beginning of January 1844, Flaubert had suddenly fallen unconscious. All he remembered later was the sense of being swept away by a 'torrent of flames'.[17] Achille, acting on the medical practice of the time, bled his brother thoroughly, but similar seizures recurred several times in the next fortnight. On one of these occasions, Flaubert's father inadvertently poured boiling water over his son's arm in an attempt to find a vein from which to bleed him, scalding him severely, scarring him for life – and temporarily preventing him from writing. What Flaubert had suffered in the carriage, as he explained in a letter to Ernest Chevalier, was a 'congestion of the brain, a kind of miniature apoplectic fit' during which he had nearly died.[18] Later, he would describe it as an illness of the memory, during which images haemorrhaged from him like blood as his mind exploded like a thousand fireworks.

Today it is generally agreed that Flaubert had suffered his first serious attack of epilepsy. In 1844, however, such a diagnosis was considered shameful: instead, Flaubert had had a 'nervous crisis'. Bedridden, forbidden wine, rich food and his beloved pipe; obliged to swallow pills and tisanes; bled, sometimes with leeches; and with an itchy, suppurating seton in his neck preventing him from moving, Flaubert felt as if he were already dead. But there was a silver lining to all this suffering. Because of his worrying state of health, the family decided he should abandon his law studies and remain at home. To his delight, Flaubert unexpectedly found himself free to pursue his dream of devoting the rest of his life to writing.

3

Deaths and Desires, 1844–8

ITALY. Must be seen immediately after marriage.
Very disappointing, not as beautiful as people say.

Gustave Flaubert, *Dictionary of Received Ideas*

For the first few months of 1844, Flaubert felt too weak to write.
His fits continued, and he could do little with his painful right
hand, though by the end of April he was able to begin using it,
with some difficulty, to shave. He envied Maxime Du Camp,
who had embarked on an extensive journey through Turkey,
Greece and Italy while he languished at home, forbidden to go
anywhere unaccompanied. Flaubert's enforced inactivity had
given him time to reflect, however, and when he resumed work
on *Sentimental Education* in May, he gave the novel a change of
tack that reflected his new situation. Rather than rework what
he had already written, he indicated that Jules' life had reached a
decisive but unspecified turning point by introducing a deliberately
mysterious encounter with a sinister dog and a vision of the
drifting, drowned corpse of the lover who had betrayed him.
From being a character whose literary pretensions were mocked
and ironized, Jules was transformed into the mouthpiece for a
new literary aesthetic. In a long final chapter, Jules reflects on
the problems that face a writer – questions that preoccupied
Flaubert – such as the difficulty of representing truth through
fiction, or of capturing life's infinite variety in words that never

seem adequate. But in depicting the mystical and all-consuming nature of Jules' literary calling, Flaubert tried above all to convey the overwhelming importance of the writer's quest:

> Reaching out to all the elements, he brings everything back to himself and puts his entire being into his vocation, into his mission, into the fatality of his genius and his labour, in a vast pantheism that passes through him to reappear in art.[1]

The novel ends with Jules leaving for the Orient, carrying with him a copy of Homer to read by the Hellespont – thus vicariously fulfilling an ambition expressed by Flaubert at the end of his Corsican journal.

In June 1844 the Flaubert family moved from their apartment in the Hôtel-Dieu to a handsome riverside property which Dr Flaubert had bought in Croisset, a village just outside Rouen. A low, white building set in a large garden, the Croisset house had once belonged to the Abbey of St Ouen. Flaubert liked to think that Pascal might once have wandered through the grounds and that it was where the Abbé Prévost had written *Manon Lescaut*. Planning to spend their winters in Rouen and summers in Croisset, the family purchased a small dinghy so that Flaubert could row or sail on the Seine, which flowed past the foot of the garden. Despite this, and despite being free to write whatever he liked, Flaubert felt bored, restless and depressed. He described himself as 'a walking shadow, a thinking ghost'; he was still too weak to do much; he missed the camaraderie of his Parisian life; and – the last straw – his favourite pipe, a present from Constantinople that he had smoked for the past seven years, had gone missing when his student belongings were returned to Rouen from Paris. Du Camp sent him letters of encouragement from abroad, but grew increasingly exasperated by his friend's self-pity. At the end of October, Du Camp wrote Flaubert a bracingly forthright letter from Rome, urging him to appreciate his good fortune in having a comfortable home, a loving family and loyal friends, and warning him of the dangers of devoting himself exclusively to a literary existence:

> art has never satisfied the heart. Remember this, Gustave; it is with the heart that one lives. It is the only thing that brings one some degree of happiness . . . It is beautiful to love art, but you must not sacrifice everything to it.[2]

Flaubert's response has not survived, but as he continued to work on *Sentimental Education*, his despair gradually faded, and by the following January he had not only accepted his new existence but had come to appreciate its merits:

> I see no one except Alfred Le Poittevin. I live alone, like a bear . . . The good thing about my illness is that I am allowed to spend my time as I please, which is a great thing in life. I can't think of anything in the world I would rather have than a nice, well-heated room, with the books one loves and all the leisure one could wish for.[3]

Meanwhile, the family provided distractions. In November 1844, Caroline's engagement to Émile Hamard was announced. On hearing the news, Flaubert simply said 'Ah' – perhaps because it came as little surprise, perhaps because he feared his close relationship with his sister would never be the same, or perhaps because he sensed a certain psychological fragility in Hamard, who had barely recovered from the recent deaths of his brother and mother. The wedding took place in March 1845, and the newly-weds moved into Hamard's Paris apartment before leaving for their Italian honeymoon a month later, accompanied by the bride's parents and Flaubert. The original plan was for the family to travel south together through Arles and Marseilles to

Genoa, from where Caroline and her husband would continue on their own to visit Florence, Rome and Naples while Flaubert and his parents toured the south of France. Flaubert intended to call on Eulalie Foucaud when they were in Marseilles, and he looked forward to exploring new places and re-experiencing the emotions that had overwhelmed him on his previous journey to the Mediterranean – but a swelling on his tongue and two major seizures marred his journey south, the weather turned cold and wet, Eulalie's hotel lay derelict, and travelling in a family group meant that he was never alone, never free to commune with his surroundings. Moreover, his father had developed a painful eye condition that needed to be treated with leeches, and Caroline's delicate health was causing concern. Flaubert felt he was undergoing what he dismissively called a grocer's experience of the Mediterranean, and in one of his regular letters home to Alfred Le Poittevin, he warned him never, ever, to travel in company.

As on his previous travels, Flaubert took notes on anything that caught his attention, from interesting faces glimpsed through the carriage window to towering piles of human bones excavated from a cemetery at Menton. In Genoa, however, one sight surpassed all others for Flaubert: in the Palazzo Stefano Balbi, he was entranced by Brueghel's painting of *The Temptation of St Anthony*, in which the saint – surrounded by crowds of grotesque creatures, part-human, part-beast – turns away from the naked women who try to caress him. For Flaubert, the painting eclipsed everything else in the gallery, and it stayed vividly in his mind, joining memories of the marionette version of the Temptation that had so enthralled him as a child. Seeing the painting started him thinking about a stage adaptation of *The Temptation of St Anthony*, but, he told Le Poittevin, someone else would have to write it.

Instead of parting company at Genoa, the group decided to stay together, since Madame Flaubert was desperately anxious about Caroline's health. Dr Flaubert talked of them all continuing

Wooden marionette of St Anthony and his pig, first half of the 19th century, France.

south to Naples, but to Flaubert's immense relief, that idea was abandoned: although he longed to see Naples, he needed to absorb its atmosphere in his own way – impossible when surrounded by family. 'Travel must be serious work,' he told Le Poittevin; 'If not, unless you spend the whole day getting drunk, it is one of the most bitter and stupid things in life.'[4] In the end, the party decided that they should all head for home, travelling via Milan, Como (where Flaubert, when no one was looking, gently kissed the marble armpit of Canova's sculpture of *Cupid and Psyche*) and Switzerland. Under his influence, perhaps, the return journey turned into something of a literary pilgrimage. Visiting the castle of Chillon, particularly resonant for Flaubert because of Byron's famous poem, he found to his dismay that graffiti on the dungeon's walls included the signatures not only of Byron but of Victor Hugo and George Sand, whom he thought should have known better. In Coppet, the party toured Madame de Staël's residence; in Geneva, they viewed Rousseau's manuscripts as well as Pradier's recent statue of the philosopher; in Ferney, they visited Voltaire's house; and in Besançon, they managed with some difficulty to locate Hugo's birthplace, which they were shown round by the godmother of the great writer. Flaubert used the Besançon visit as an excuse to call on the Hugo household when the family passed through Paris on their way back to Normandy, but Madame Hugo gave the young man a frosty reception.

Although the Italian trip had not been an unqualified success, the long periods spent cooped up in a slow-moving coach had given Flaubert time to reflect on the next stage of his life, and once back in Croisset, he was content to live 'like an oyster in its shell',[5] studying Greek, reading classical history, rereading his beloved Shakespeare and planning to write an Oriental tale. His health had not improved – an outbreak of painful, suppurating boils added to his discomfort – and the household seemed dull without Caroline to enliven it, but while he noticed that he rarely laughed any more, he did not really feel unhappy. Passion and action were not for him, he decided: if happiness lay anywhere, it was in stagnation.

Shortly after his 24th birthday, however, this period of calm resignation came to an abrupt end. Dr Flaubert developed a large abscess on his thigh, and it soon became clear that surgery was required. The operation was performed by his son, Achille, but septicaemia quickly set in, and on 15 January 1846, Dr Flaubert died at home in the Hôtel-Dieu. Achille-Cléophas

James Pradier, *Achille-Cléophas Flaubert*, 1847, marble bust.

was greatly mourned. The local newspaper called on the community to raise a subscription for his tombstone and erect a statue in grateful memory of their distinguished doctor, and the townspeople of Rouen turned out in huge numbers for the funeral. But the sudden loss of this gentle, intelligent, loving and cultured man came as an even more devastating blow to his family and Flaubert feared that his mother would die of grief.

Worse was to follow, however. At the same family apartment in the Hôtel-Dieu, barely five days after Achille-Cléophas' death, Caroline gave birth to a daughter who was also given the ill-fated name of Caroline. When the baby was only a few days old, Flaubert's sister developed a high fever. Although she seemed briefly to recover and doctors assured the family at the end of January that she was out of danger, she soon relapsed in agony, and it became evident that she would not survive. 'You were born in the midst of tears. That brought you unhappiness,' Flaubert told his niece many years later.[6] On 15 March he described the sorrowing household to Du Camp:

> Hamard has just left my room, where he stood by the fireplace, sobbing. My mother is a weeping statue. Caroline talks, smiles, caresses us, says sweet and affectionate words to us all. She is losing her memory; everything is muddled in her head . . . The baby suckles and cries. Achille says nothing and does not know what to say. What a house! What a hell![7]

In his own grief for the sister he adored, Flaubert remained dry-eyed. He observed his reaction with interest and noted that while he might be overwhelmed by fictional pain, true grief made his heart hard and bitter. Experience had taught him survival strategies. As he advised a friend at this time, it was best to detach oneself from potential suffering: 'Stay as you are for ever, do not marry, do not have children, have as few attachments as possible, offer as little purchase as possible to the enemy.'[8]

Caroline died, aged 21, on 22 March 1846. After her corpse had been dressed in her wedding gown and long veil, Flaubert sat by it throughout the night, reading Montaigne. In the morning, stooping to give his sister a last farewell kiss, he felt the lead of the coffin bend as he leaned against it. He cut a lock of her hair as a keepsake and watched as clumsy practitioners took plaster casts of her hand and face. She was to be buried next to her father. Once again, the funeral cortège wound its slow way through the streets of Rouen and up to the cemetery high above the town. There, the freshly dug grave proved too narrow for the coffin. Gravediggers pushed, pulled and tilted it to no avail, before resorting to spades and levers as the mourners watched and Caroline's distraught widower fell sobbing to his knees by the open grave. Finally, one of the gravediggers stamped hard on the coffin above where Caroline's head must have lain, and forced it down into the hole. Flaubert looked on in silent fury but remained 'as dry as a tombstone', before returning to Croisset by carriage with his weeping mother and the crying baby. The following day he wrote to Du Camp with an account of the funeral's grotesque details, adding, 'I wanted to tell you all this because I thought it would give you pleasure,' confident that his writer friend would understand and know that he did not mean 'pleasure' in the common, 'bourgeois' sense of the word.[9]

In the aftermath of the devastating double bereavement, there was much for Flaubert to do. The baby's baptism had to be arranged – though the symbolism of the church ceremony had little meaning for her uncle, who felt as if he were witnessing the rituals of some long-dead religion. Legal steps had to be taken to give Madame Flaubert custody of little Caroline, for Hamard's fragile mental health had broken down completely, and he could not be trusted with the baby. Flaubert also needed to find winter lodgings in Rouen for himself, his mother and his niece, since Achille had been appointed to his father's post at the Hôtel-Dieu, despite some opposition, and with his wife and young daughter had been allocated the family's former accommodation. A suitable house was eventually found nearby on rue Crosne-hors-Ville, since renamed avenue Gustave Flaubert. There was work to be done, too, in drumming up public support for the proposed bust of Dr Flaubert, which was to be sculpted by James Pradier, whom Flaubert had also commissioned to produce a bust of his sister from her death mask.

Sharing a house with his grieving mother and the new baby proved oppressive. Whenever he could, Flaubert immersed himself in his work, shutting himself in his study for eight to ten hours a day in order to read ancient history or to write.

Even a brief disturbance could make him feel unwell, and although he still dreamed of distant travel on horseback, days passed without him setting foot outdoors. When he learned in June that Alfred Le Poittevin was about to marry Louise de Maupassant and move to Paris after an Italian honeymoon, he received his friend's happy news as yet another personal blow. 'It's another loss for me,' he told Ernest Chevalier, 'and doubly so, first because he is getting married and then because he is going to live elsewhere. Everything passes! Everything passes!'[10]

That summer, Flaubert's life underwent another major change. Having gone to Paris at the end of July to discuss the commissions with Pradier, in the sculptor's studio he noticed a strikingly attractive woman in a blue gown. Her name was Louise Colet. Eleven years his senior, she was a prolific and award-winning writer, married to a professional flautist. For several years, however, she had been the mistress of the eminent philosopher Victor Cousin, who was widely rumoured to be the father of her daughter, Henriette. By the day after their first meeting, Louise and Flaubert had become lovers. The following evening they drove together through the Bois de Boulogne with five-year-old Henriette asleep on cushions beside them, and watched as the sky blazed with fireworks celebrating the anniversary of the July Revolution of 1830. When Flaubert finally left Paris on 4 August, Louise accompanied him to the station and wept as they parted; stepping off the train in Rouen, he found his mother waiting anxiously for him on the platform, weeping tears of relief at his return.

That evening, back in Croisset and surrounded by mementos of Louise – her little slippers, two billets-doux, a portrait and a perfumed, blood-stained handkerchief – Flaubert wrote her a letter, taking care not to use his black-edged mourning paper because, he said, he wanted nothing sad to pass between them:

I should like to cause you nothing but joy, and to enfold
you in calm, continuous happiness, in some small
recompense for everything you have so freely given me
in the generosity of your love.[11]

The love letters he sent her over the next few days were long
and confusingly ambivalent, a mixture of sexual desire, distancing
tactics and posturing self-analysis. Louise's arrival in his life
disrupted everything – he told her that he could no longer read,
think or write – but from the outset he warned her that he was
cold and selfish and would bring her only unhappiness. 'I can see
that you are suffering,' he wrote to her barely a week after their
first meeting, 'and I foresee that I shall make you suffer. For your
sake and for mine I should like never to have known you, and yet
the thought of you attracts me irresistibly.'[12] He loved her and
desired her, yet he felt incapable of the intensity of passion she
seemed to expect of him; she had sworn to love him forever, but
that was not a promise he could make in return, for he knew that
happiness never lasted. Louise had stirred up the stagnant pond
that was his previous existence, and when disturbed, he warned her,
such ponds invariably give off an unhealthy stench. In an attempt
to explain why his emotional responses were in such disarray,
he related Herodotus' tale of how the ancient Numidians seared
their children's scalps with hot coals to desensitize them to the
burning heat of the sun; he had been raised like a Numidian child,
he claimed, and so could no longer feel. Yet he signed that letter
'A thousand kisses, a thousand, everywhere, *everywhere*.'[13] Louise
reacted to his mixed messages by becoming more demanding: he
was to write to her at least once a day, he was to drop everything
and come to live in Paris, and they were to write a book together.
   Terrified that his mother might discover their relationship,
Flaubert pretended that the letters arriving daily for him came from
Maxime Du Camp, and when Du Camp was due to visit, he instructed

Louise to maintain the deception by putting Du Camp's name on the envelopes she sent to the Croisset address. The subterfuges continued: he asked Pradier to send a letter summoning him to Paris as a pretext to visit Louise; he arranged a rendezvous with her in Mantes while pretending to be with Du Camp; he promised visits, but then cancelled because his mother needed him. 'Her suffering imposes a thousand unimaginable tyrannies on me,' he told Louise, who reacted with tears and fury, accusing him of being watched over like a young girl.[14] For several anxious weeks, he feared that she was pregnant, and when she wrote to say it had been a false alarm, he responded, 'That's good, it means one less wretch on earth. One less victim to boredom, vice or crime, and certainly to misfortune.'[15]

The exchange of letters continued almost daily. On Flaubert's side, it was an outpouring of passion and tender intimacy, interspersed with discussions of literature and rebuttals of Louise's increasingly jealous accusations. She was jealous of his mother, jealous of Du Camp, jealous of Eulalie Foucaud, whom Flaubert had recently tried to contact in Cayenne, and jealous of the promiscuous and alluring Louise Pradier, now separated from her husband.

Matters came to a head in February 1847, when Flaubert received the shocking news that an exploding gas lamp had killed an old school friend, Félix d'Arcet, Louise Pradier's brother, as he lay in bed in Brazil. Flaubert immediately travelled to Paris to see Pradier and the d'Arcet family. Louise Colet was incensed when she discovered that he had visited the capital without telling her, and in a blazing row that precipitated another of Flaubert's nervous seizures, she accused him of lying and of being Louise Pradier's lover. Although the angry scene brought that first phase of their turbulent relationship to an end, the pair continued to exchange letters of recrimination and self-justification. As he frequently did, Flaubert resorted to medical imagery to explain himself, telling Louise that, like the wrinkled, mummified skin of his burned hand, his soul had passed through fire and was equally insensitive.

Adèle Grasset, *Louise Colet and Her Daughter Henriette*, 1842, oil on canvas.

'In my case, think of it as an infirmity,' he urged her, 'a shameful internal sickness I caught from being around unhealthy things; but don't be upset about it, for there is nothing to be done.'[16]

In the meantime, Flaubert had made plans that did not involve Louise. On 1 May 1847 he and Du Camp embarked on their long-anticipated travels – not the great Oriental journey that Flaubert had dreamed of, but a three-month tour of Brittany to which Madame Flaubert had finally given reluctant consent. Their route followed a carefully planned itinerary, taking them past the châteaux of the Loire and round the coast of Brittany from south to north, with many forays into the interior. They travelled by train, stagecoach, steamboat, rowing boat, carriage, omnibus and cart, but more than 640 km (400 miles) of the journey were covered on foot. To the two city-dwellers, the farther reaches of Breton-speaking Brittany seemed wonderfully alien, a primitive region of poverty and superstition that remained rooted in the past, while to the locals, the two young travellers with packs on their backs and staffs in their hands were figures of curiosity and deep suspicion. Irked at the frequency with which officials demanded to inspect his passport, Flaubert convinced one particularly intrusive customs officer that he and his companion were on a secret mission from the king.

Travelling conditions were not easy. Writing to Ernest Chevalier, Flaubert complained of fleas, grim weather, poor food and having to sleep fully dressed. The sight of dolmens and menhirs began to pall, and he grumbled that all Celtic archaeology looked boringly similar. For Flaubert, the real joy of the excursion was the sense of freedom it brought:

> The sea! The sea! Open air, fields, freedom, I mean real freedom – the kind that consists of saying what one likes, thinking out loud together, and going where one's fancy takes one, letting time pass without caring more than one cares about the smoke drifting from one's pipe.[17]

His family responsibilities still weighed, however. Knowing that his mother missed him and worried about him, he agreed that she and Caroline should join them in Brest for a few days and accompany them by coach for the next part of the route. It was in Brest that the little girl took her first steps.

As they travelled, Flaubert and Du Camp noted down their impressions. Their aim was to produce a volume recording their experiences of Brittany, each writing alternate chapters. They had no thought of publishing their travelogue, and indeed the previous August, Flaubert had told Louise Colet that under no circumstances would he ever publish anything. With no wish to be constrained by external expectations or demands, he had sworn to write for himself only; writing was an intimate, personal activity, like sleeping or smoking, and the thought of writing for financial gain was anathema to him.

After reworking his notes on his return, Flaubert produced a piece of travel literature unlike any other. Du Camp was baffled, for Flaubert was excited by trivial details that were of no apparent interest. Rather than describe the Brittany of guidebooks, he preferred to focus on banal or eccentric features of everyday life such as the burial of a local sailor drowned at sea or an encounter with a soldier facing a one-year sentence for selling a pair of trousers. Moreover, he treated famous tourist sites such as Carnac's megalithic stones with amused irony, imagining the ancient boulders laughing into their lichen beards at the imbeciles who came to gape at unlovely lumps of granite. Already Flaubert was trying out descriptive and narrative techniques that were to become hallmarks of his mature style. A curbing of lyrical tendencies, an absence of explanation, suggestive but uncommented juxtapositions, subtle irony – all are evident in Flaubert's chapters of the account that he and Du Camp eventually decided to call *Over Strand and Field* (*Par les champs et par les grèves*).

During the trip itself, however, Flaubert's thoughts also turned to future projects, particularly to the possibility of writing a *Temptation of St Anthony*. Nor could he dismiss Louise Colet from his mind. He thought more fondly of her as time went on, and sent her letters that grew increasingly warm and pleading: she was the first and only woman ever to have loved him, and he had never meant to hurt her; if he had treated her harshly, it was because he had been tired and ill; he had behaved towards her, he now realized, like a surgeon trying to bandage his patient while wearing gloves of iron. In a romantic gesture, he sent her a flower he had picked at sunset on Chateaubriand's as-yet-empty tomb on the tidal island of Grand Bé. What he did not realize was that Louise had already found a new, Polish, lover and was now pregnant, a fact she would not disclose to Flaubert until shortly before the birth.

The friends' Breton itinerary was cut short in its final stages when Flaubert received an anxious summons from his mother. On her return to Croisset, Madame Flaubert had discovered that an epidemic of childhood diseases was sweeping the area and she had fled with Caroline to rented accommodation in La Bouille, some 25 km (15 miles) downriver from Rouen. She urgently wanted Flaubert to join them there, and so two weeks earlier than planned, Flaubert and Du Camp were back on familiar territory, reaching Trouville on foot at two o'clock in the morning of 24 July. Returning to the resort where he had spent many happy summers with his family, Flaubert was dismayed to find that the Trouville he held so dear had changed to such an extent that he had difficulty finding his way around. It was a painful discovery, for he associated Trouville with the happiest moments of his youth. Two days later, he and Du Camp sailed back up the Seine by steamship from Honfleur on a voyage that, for Flaubert, brought back poignant memories of similar trips with his late sister or with Alfred Le Poittevin, whom he now knew to be gravely ill. The two friends finally parted company at La Bouille, and for the next six weeks, Flaubert reluctantly stayed with his mother and niece in the 'dump' that Madame Flaubert had rented.

After the freedom of travelling with Du Camp, he found it hard to return to family life. He shut himself away in his room to read and write, but when he came down to dinner he had to face his mother's melancholy sighs and Caroline's tantrums. Anxieties crowded in: worry about money, about the health of his mother – who had started to suffer from nervous attacks and hallucinations rather like his own – and about vulnerable little Caroline, whose father had suddenly turned up from England and needed to be watched constantly in case he harmed the child with his alarmingly rough play. But above all, Flaubert was anxious about Alfred Le Poittevin. His own health began to suffer, with more seizures and visual disturbances and outbreaks of painful carbuncles that prevented him from sleeping.

Meanwhile there was unrest in the wider world too, as demands for electoral reform grew increasingly insistent across France. Although Flaubert had previously shown little interest in politics, on Christmas Day 1847, he accompanied Maxime Du Camp and Louis Bouilhet, a former classmate, to one of the reform banquets that had become a popular means of mobilizing political support for the cause. The dinner in Rouen was attended by 1,800 supporters and lasted for nine hours. Flaubert found the event grotesque, and was appalled by the pomposity of the cliché-ridden speeches, which he described in a letter to Louise Colet:

> I remained unmoved, feeling sick with disgust in the midst of the patriotic fervour roused by the tiller of State, our headlong rush towards the abyss, the honour of our flag, the shade of our ensigns, the fraternity of nations, and other mouthfuls of the same sort.[18]

When the government banned reform banquets in February 1848, however, and unrest turned to violence in Paris, Flaubert travelled to the capital to join Bouilhet and Du Camp in witnessing the closing stages of a revolution that brought Louis Philippe's eighteen-year reign to an abrupt end. For Flaubert, the revolution was more of a spectacle than a question of political engagement. He watched as the Tuileries Palace was sacked, heard volleys of gunshot without realizing what the noise meant and witnessed a new French Republic being declared at the Hôtel de Ville. But his main concern was whether the new government would be favourable to art, and everything he had seen was stored in his memory for potential use in a future novel.

For Flaubert, however, the excitement of those February days was soon eclipsed by the slow and agonizing death of Alfred Le Poittevin a few weeks later. The loss of this lifelong soulmate, whose family had been so closely entwined with his own, affected him profoundly. He kept watch by Alfred's corpse all night, reading Creuzer's *The Religions of Antiquity*, and then helped prepare his friend's body for burial. Writing to Du Camp a few days later, he spared no detail of the physical process – the sensation of Alfred's cold, stiff limbs, the body's state of putrefaction, the fluids that soaked through sheets and shroud. Setting it down in writing was a way of coping with grief and with his desperate sense of loss. To Ernest Chevalier he wrote, 'That's one less, yet another one gone, everything is collapsing around me.'[19]

4

The Orient, 1848–51

ORIENTALIST. Man who has travelled a lot.

Gustave Flaubert, *Dictionary of Received Ideas*

During his travels through Brittany, Flaubert had given more thought to *The Temptation of St Anthony*. He knew that far more research into ancient religions would be needed before he could start to write about the third-century anchorite, and so in the months following Alfred's death, he buried himself in the project. In June 1848, however, its progress was interrupted by another family crisis. Émile Hamard had reappeared in Rouen, 'completely mad' and intent on reclaiming his two-year-old daughter.[1] Terrified of what might happen, Flaubert and his mother hurriedly left home on 21 June and went into hiding, fleeing with Caroline to Forges-les-Bains, southwest of Paris, without disclosing their destination even to Achille. Hamard's uncle initiated proceedings to have the man forcibly detained in an asylum, but before the authorities could reach him, Hamard vanished.

While the family was in hiding, uncertain what to do next and with Madame Flaubert trembling at the sound of every approaching carriage, civil unrest again flared in Paris. On 22 June thousands of citizens, angered by the sudden disbanding of the National Workshop scheme that had provided them with work and wages, took to the streets in a spontaneous uprising against the provisional government. Hundreds of barricades were thrown up to block boulevards, and the demonstrations grew violent. The following day, the government declared Paris to be in a state of siege and summoned the National Guard to restore order by military force. In a brutal crackdown that continued until 26 June, 1,500 revolutionaries were killed and some 12,000 arrested.

Word reached Flaubert that Maxime Du Camp had been shot in the leg during an assault on one of the barricades, and anxiety about his friend added to his worries. The immediate concern over Caroline's future was temporarily resolved, however, when Hamard's lawyer agreed that she could remain with her grandmother until January, pending a legal inquiry to determine who should have custody. But wherever Flaubert looked, he could see only troubles – 'worries, dread, ruin, sadness, death' – a bleakness compounded by news that Chateaubriand, the great Romantic writer to whose Breton birthplace and empty tomb he had made a pilgrimage the previous year, had passed away during the national turmoil.[2]

Like many at the time, Flaubert feared that France would soon dissolve into civil war; he had a powerful old rifle renovated in case he needed to use it. But what he feared even more than civil war, he told Ernest Chevalier, was becoming engulfed in yet another family drama: 'Oh, families – what a bloody nuisance! What a mess! What a ball and chain! How they engulf you – you rot there and die a living death!'[3] Flaubert was relieved of one pressing family worry in January 1849, however, when a tribunal ruled that Caroline should remain in the care of the Flauberts. Moreover, by the spring of that year he was looking forward to an even greater release from family constraints. He and Du Camp had drawn up a plan to set off on their travels again, but this time, they intended to go much further, and for much longer. Their aim was to spend about a year and a half travelling through 'all the Orient', the combined efforts of Achille and Dr Cloquet having finally persuaded Madame Flaubert that the hot climate would be beneficial for her son's health.

Flaubert was determined to finish *The Temptation of St Anthony* before they left. Although he had already carried out extensive research into the ancient religions and history of the East, he found writing it to be a laborious process. In September, however, he finally completed his manuscript and summoned Bouilhet and Du Camp to hear him read it aloud. Neither knew quite what to expect, but both assumed it would be a scholarly examination of the period surrounding the rise of the early Christian Church and the collapse of the Roman Empire. But Flaubert's semi-dramatized narrative of the myriad heretics, fantastical beasts, lubricious women and ancient gods that dominate Anthony's visions was far removed from conventional history. Instead of producing an erudite reconstruction of antiquity, he had used his researches as a springboard to free his imagination to soar, like Anthony's, far beyond the deserts of ancient Egypt. For eight hours a day over a period of four days, he read the work aloud to his friends, and then waited eagerly for their reaction. When it came, it was brutally frank: they advised him to throw the manuscript in the fire and never mention it again.

To Bouilhet and Du Camp, the work seemed a meaningless string of beautifully constructed sentences, full of grandiose images and strange metaphors but with no coherence, development or conclusion. They felt that Flaubert had been carried away by his own lyricism and advised him instead to find a contemporary, down-to-earth subject that would force him to keep his lyrical tendencies in check. Having his trusted friends so categorically dismiss a project he had mulled over for years was a devastating blow for Flaubert. He felt that his entire *raison d'être* had been destroyed.

Within days of the crushing verdict, however, Flaubert and Du Camp set off on their great Oriental adventure. Behind them they left a distraught Madame Flaubert, who on parting from her son let out a piercing cry of grief that reminded Flaubert of the terrible scream she had uttered at his father's deathbed. Mother and son both sobbed alone that evening, but Flaubert soon settled into the journey's rhythm. To facilitate their reception in the countries they were to pass through, Du Camp had secured a somewhat spurious commission from the Ministry of Education, while Flaubert, preposterously, carried an official document from the Ministry of Agriculture that charged him with gathering commercial information during the trip. They sent two large trunks on ahead with 310 kg (680 lbs) of equipment, including saddles, camp beds, a large tent, a table, a medicine chest and two musical snuffboxes, while Flaubert's remaining luggage contained paper, ink and volumes of Herodotus and Homer. Accompanying them on the journey was Du Camp's valet, Louis Sassetti, a good-natured and resourceful young Corsican who had already spent time in Egypt. The three men sailed from Marseilles on 4 November 1849, and after a refuelling stop at Malta that was prolonged because of rough seas, their ship docked at Alexandria eleven days later.

Flaubert's imagination had long been steeped in the Romantic Orient of popular fantasy – an illusory amalgam of exotic scents, rich jewels, gleaming minarets and voluptuous, dark-eyed beauties – but he had read enough to know that the reality would be different, and he travelled with an open mind. Alexandria was too full of Europeans to seem truly foreign, but in Cairo there were fewer men in top hats: Cairo, with its active slave market and its bazaars with camels lying between the stalls was where he felt the Orient really began. The landscape, the vegetation and the desert were as he had expected from his reading, but as he told Bouilhet, 'I am discovering everything else for the first time. But there is a new element which I did not expect to see and which is immense here: it is the grotesque.'[4]

Flaubert's sensibility had long been attuned to the grotesque, and now he noted it everywhere: in the blackened intestines spilling out of a half-eaten camel carcass lying in the desert; in the child in dusty Mahatta so deformed by rickets that his spine seemed broken; in the tale of the Turk and his horse, both devoured by jackals near the Nile's first cataract the previous year; and in countless other details that he recorded. But there were also moments of sublime beauty. Nearing the pyramids on horseback late one afternoon, he and his companions spurred their mounts and galloped across the desert to the foot of the Great Sphinx. As they approached, it seemed to rise up out of the ground, bathed in a pink glow from the setting sun, and Flaubert, who had brought an imaginary sphinx to life in his ill-fated *Temptation of St Anthony*, was overcome with emotion.

For the more practical Du Camp, one of the expedition's aims was to make a photographic record of the ancient monuments they saw. In 1849 photography was still in its infancy. It was only ten years since Louis Daguerre had presented his new invention to the French Academy of Sciences, but Du Camp had taken lessons in calotype photography from the pioneering photographer Gustave Le Gray in preparation for the journey, and had gone to great trouble to pack his heavy photographic equipment and chemicals so as to protect them from being damaged while jolting along on the back of a camel or a mule. Setting up the equipment was a lengthy process, but as seen through Flaubert's eyes, it was also macabre: Du Camp's head disappearing into the 'black shroud' of the photographic tent seemed like a decapitation. Although Flaubert would later be deeply scornful of photography, his letters from Egypt show him taking an appreciative interest in his friend's photographic attempts and helping out on at least one occasion that left his his fingers stained black with silver nitrate. Du Camp managed to bring over two hundred images back to France, and in 1852 he published *Egypt, Nubia, Palestine and Syria*, a volume containing 125 prints taken on their journey and the first book about the region ever to be illustrated with photographs. One of the images showed the partially excavated Sphinx, thus putting paid to a widespread belief that the mysterious, huge head that rose out of the desert had no body.

On the night the travellers reached the Sphinx, they slept under canvas for the first time, while jackals howled in the distance. Their Arab guides wrapped themselves in blankets and lay in hollows scooped in the desert sand, looking to Flaubert 'like cadavers in their shrouds'.[5] The following morning, he and Du Camp rose before dawn to climb the Great Pyramid of Giza. It was a more challenging climb than Flaubert expected. The guides – two in front and two behind – had to push and pull their breathless client up the massive blocks of stone, but he and Du Camp reached the summit in time to see the sun rise. Watching the landscape change as day broke made a deep impression on Flaubert, and he tried to capture every detail of the effects in his notebook – the low band of orange sky, the pale desert gradually giving way to an ocean of violet sand, a distant network of canals and tufted palm trees emerging from darkness. Years later, his description in *Salammbô* of sunrise over Carthage would owe much to that Egyptian dawn viewed from the top of an ancient pyramid.

The Sphinx and the great Pyramid of Menkaure, photographed by Maxime Du Camp, 1849.

When he visited the pyramid's interior, however, slithering over bat droppings and crawling on all fours along narrow passages, Flaubert was annoyed to find evidence of his compatriots' vandalism. Previous visitors – 'imbeciles' – had scrawled their names all over the walls; one Frenchman even announced himself as a wallpaper manufacturer and included his address. But when Flaubert climbed down into an ancient tomb at Saqqara, where the ground was littered with fragments of human bone, and found pots containing mummified ibis lined up in neat rows 'like sugar loaves in a grocer's shop', he had no qualms about collecting half a dozen to take back to Normandy as souvenirs, though only one survived the journey.[6] He contemplated also bringing home a human mummy, but the logistics defeated him.

Not all his Cairo excursions involved archaeological sites. Flaubert was also interested in visiting local hospitals. He sought out a civil hospital for the insane, and toured a military hospital where the doctor showing him round ordered a ward full of patients with advanced venereal disease to display their hideous lesions, causing him to reel back at the stench. In the anatomy theatre, where a half-dissected cadaver lay on the slab, he recognized anatomical diagrams and a papier mâché Auzoux model of a foetus that were familiar to him from his childhood in the Hôtel-Dieu. On at least two occasions he met doctors who were familiar with his father's medical work, giving him a comforting sense of his father's presence protecting him on his travels.

Flaubert and Du Camp remained in Cairo for two and a half months, exploring the city and its environs and soon becoming acquainted with some of its large French population. Every detail of Egyptian life fascinated or amused Flaubert, and he made vivid notes. These were for his private use, for although he had promised to contribute articles about his travels to the *Revue de l'Orient*, the humiliating reception of *The Temptation of St Anthony* had changed his mind. As he told Dr Cloquet in a letter from Cairo, he was 'firmly resolved *to publish nothing* for a very long time'.[7]

The friends left Cairo on 6 February 1850, and for the next six weeks they sailed up the Nile towards its furthest navigable point, the second cataract, 1,600 km (1,000 miles) from the delta. The heat was blistering. From time to time they disembarked to collect or send mail, buy provisions, explore the immediate surroundings, shoot at hyenas, birds and crocodiles (usually missing them) and visit brothels. Once, they passed two boats carrying tattooed women whose Arab slave-masters tried to sell them gourds. For the most part, however, they relaxed on board, smoking hookahs, sipping lemonade and gazing at the passing scenery. Flaubert often slept for fifteen hours at a stretch on the hard bed that doubled as a writing table during the day, and he noticed that he was putting on weight at an alarming rate. Thoughts of serious composition were set aside for the time being: 'It is better simply to be an eye,' he commented.[8] Instead, he spent his mornings reading Homer in Greek, and his evenings recording what he had seen during the day and writing long letters home. The letters to his mother were full of affectionate reassurance and travel descriptions, but in those to Bouilhet he included flamboyant accounts of his many sexual exploits along the way.

The most memorable of these took place at Esna, where a veiled servant girl with hennaed hands came on board, preceded by a pet lamb in a black velvet muzzle. She led Flaubert and Du Camp to the house of Kuchuk-Hanem, a local courtesan renowned for her erotic inventiveness, who perfumed their hands with rosewater before performing a sequence of sensual dances, including the famous 'dance of the bee'. Flaubert was fascinated by her – by her scent, her flesh, her gauzy garments, her gold jewellery and her strange headdress with its dangling beads, and by the mysterious line of blue script tattooed on her right arm.

They spent the night together, with her little dog curled up asleep on his silk jacket. Lying drowsily beside Kuchuk-Hanem as she slept, however, Flaubert found his mind wandering to thoughts of Judith's beheading of Holofernes. He sent Bouilhet a lengthy and graphic account of the exotic, erotic experience, and made detailed notes in his journal, knowing that they might prove useful in the future. Flaubert and Du Camp stopped again at Esna on the way back, but Kuchuk-Hanem's servant now had a bandaged eye, the lamb had died, and Kuchuk-Hanem herself looked tired and ill. Although she danced for them, and Flaubert again shared her bed, the second encounter left him with a deep sense of melancholy.

The return journey down the Nile went at a leisurely pace, with many stops and excursions, including two weeks spent exploring the ruins of Thebes and an arduous four-day trek by camel and on foot across the baking desert to Kosseir on the Red Sea coast, which nearly ended in disaster when a camel stumbled and fell, crushing their water bottles. With nothing to drink, they resorted to sucking fragments of stone, but grew increasingly parched and desperate in the heat. To Du Camp's fury, Flaubert began to fantasize about swallowing a spoonful of lemon sorbet and refused to stop describing its cool, thirst-quenching delights. It was one of the moments that strained their relationship, just as Flaubert's tendency to prolong a joke well beyond its limits would test the patience of friends throughout his life.

On 25 June, Flaubert and Du Camp arrived back in Cairo, where they packed up trunk-loads of possessions to send back to Rouen before sailing on to Alexandria. Flaubert was sorry to leave Egypt, and he regretted having been unable to continue up the Nile into the very heart of Africa, into 'the land of monkeys and elephants'.[9] But the Nile expedition had lasted over four and a half months and, as he noted with satisfaction, few European visitors had explored the country as thoroughly as he and Du Camp had done.

The next stage of their itinerary took them by boat to Beirut, and then on horseback down the coast of Lebanon and into Palestine. From Jaffa (which smelled to Flaubert like a mixture of lemon blossom and half-rotted corpses) they turned inland to Jerusalem, with excursions to Bethlehem and the Dead Sea, and then north to Nablus and Nazareth, before crossing into Syria. Their original plan had been to travel on to Persia, but the journey was proving expensive, and so, after spending eleven days in Damascus and visiting the ruins of Baalbek, they turned for home, sailing from Beirut on 1 October.

More than nine months of travel still lay ahead of them, however. The return journey took them first to Rhodes, and then on horseback from Marmaris to Smyrna via Ephesus. From Smyrna they caught a steamship that took them through the Dardanelles to Constantinople, where they remained for over a month. It was there that Flaubert learned, to his sorrow, of the death of Balzac, whose novels he greatly admired and whom he had hoped one day to meet. From Turkey they travelled onwards to visit ancient sites in Greece – the Athens Acropolis, Thermopylae, Delphi, Corinth, Sparta, Olympia and Patras – and then to Italy. They landed at Brindisi on 17 February, and set off by coach for Naples, where Flaubert was greatly taken by Caravaggio's painting of *Judith Beheading Holofernes*. The blood, he noted, was the right colour – dark reddish-brown rather than the deep purple often used by painters – and he admired its truth. On the way, they made excursions to Vesuvius, Herculaneum, Paestum and Pompeii, before reaching Rome on 29 March 1851. There the two friends finally parted.

Although they had enjoyed French government hospitality at various points on their journey, for much of the time Flaubert and Du Camp had travelled in great discomfort – saddle-sore, weather-beaten and plagued by mosquitoes, lice, bedbugs and fleas. They endured sandstorms and tempests, searing heat and bitter cold. They coped with swamps and floods, mists and hail, and in Greece, they lost their way in deep snow. Illness was a frequent concern: Flaubert, Du Camp and Sassetti all contracted venereal diseases on the journey, and at various stages all suffered from fevers, digestive disorders and severe exhaustion. There were other discomforts, too, including wayward camels, bolting horses, disintegrating footwear, inedible food and a narrow escape in Palestine when they were repeatedly shot at by a group of Bedouins. But despite the length and rigours of the journey, Flaubert did not want it to end. No sooner had they reached Rome than he was longing to return to the Orient or visit the Pampas of South America, the Sudan or the East Indies. Travel, he told Ernest Chevalier, was the most intense form of debauchery.

The friends had designed their itinerary to let them explore and record as many ancient sites as possible, and Flaubert's already deep knowledge of antiquity was further expanded by visits to museums in the cities through which they passed. He was particularly moved by the Acropolis in Athens, and like much else on the journey, the site and the flowing drapery of its sculptures left a profound impression on his literary imagination. If he later compared the thankless process of literary production to the way in which the Egyptian pyramids were laboriously constructed, block by block, and then abandoned in the desert to be clambered over by bourgeois sightseers and pissed on by jackals, the Parthenon, too, came to represent the writing process: some of its stones, he noted, were the colour of ink, and the precision of its construction, the smoothness of its surface and its overall harmony came to symbolize for him the type of perfection he sought to achieve in his writing. Flaubert felt that his visit to the Acropolis had justified the entire journey, and in 'an Olympian state, inhaling antiquity till [his] brain was full of it', he pocketed two pieces of marble from the Parthenon to take home to Croisset.[10]

Fascinated as he was by antiquity, however, visiting ancient ruins could pall. In Egypt, he balked at the prospect of viewing the remains of yet another temple; Jerusalem's old city reminded him of a fortified charnel house; and tourist graffiti continued to mar the atmosphere of many sites, most glaringly at Pompey's Pillar in Alexandria, which bore the name of a certain Mr Thompson from Sunderland in letters 1.8 m (6 ft) high. On the other hand, Flaubert never ceased to be fascinated by the local people he encountered on his travels. He enjoyed their conversation and delighted in watching their quarrels, mannerisms and dress. Having constant opportunities to observe 'the psychological, human, comic side' of life was a welcome aspect of travel that he had not anticipated.[11] Yet although the journey brought him a wealth of new sights and experiences, he found that travel often induced in him a melancholy, somnolent state in which his mind wandered while sounds and landscapes drifted by. As he explained to his mother,

> On horseback, one's mind jogs steadily down all the byways of thought; it travels back into memories, stopping at crossroads and forks in the path, trampling dead leaves underfoot and poking its nose over fences.[12]

Despite his extraordinary and unfamiliar surroundings, then, Flaubert's thoughts frequently turned inward, particularly to Normandy and to family and friends he would never see again.

It irked Du Camp that with exotic scenery before his eyes, Flaubert dreamed of Norman landscapes, but what he failed to appreciate was that Flaubert's thoughts of Normandy were starting to take on new significance as he continued to contemplate his future. In Smyrna, he had read a novel of manners by the prolific and immensely popular Eugène Sue, which had confirmed his view that French literature was in a pitiful state – diseased, moribund. 'It would take Christs of Art to cure that leper,' he declared.[13] Did Flaubert already see himself as such a saviour, come to restore a literary tradition to health? From Constantinople, he wrote to Bouilhet that the solution to literature's problems was not to look back to antiquity or the Middle Ages – that had already been done – but to focus on the present. He now felt a real need to establish himself as a writer, and as he continued on his travels, ideas for a novel set in contemporary Normandy began to take shape in his mind.

Du Camp was not an encouraging audience for these ideas, and Flaubert needed encouragement. His confidence fluctuated: at times he felt utterly defeated, but occasionally a surging sense of literary potential left him in a state of exhilaration. Before leaving Cairo he had felt an explosion of intellectual intensity – as he reported to Bouilhet, 'the pot suddenly started to boil, and I felt a burning need to write.'[14] Various ideas for subjects came to him: he might pursue an earlier scheme for a *Dictionary of Received Ideas*, organized so that readers would be unable to tell whether they were being mocked, or he might write about Don Juan, or Anubis, or a young woman living and dying in a small provincial backwater, or perhaps he would compose a play ('very brutal, very farcical and of course very impartial') about contemporary politics and society. By the time he reached Greece his literary confidence had waned, but that he *would* continue to write was no longer in question: 'What am I going to write when I get home? That's what I ask myself constantly.'[15]

Madame Flaubert was equally concerned about what her son would do on his return, and wrote to suggest he consider taking 'a little job that would not involve much and would not prevent [him] from doing other things'. Flaubert's reply was robust: he was incapable of holding down any post; it was ridiculous to expect someone to work all day and write poetry after dinner; he could manage perfectly well without a job, which in any case would only earn him a pittance; his mother must abandon this futile notion.

But despite his outrage, Flaubert missed his mother and worried about how she was faring without him. In March 1850, he had written to her from Egypt:

Do you know that we are nearly fourteen hundred leagues apart! . . . Sometimes the desire to see you grips me suddenly

like a spasm of tenderness . . . it's in the evening before going
to sleep that I think of you a lot; and every morning when I
wake up you are the first thing that comes into my mind.[16]

By November 1850 it was agreed that Madame Flaubert would join
her son in Italy the following spring. Caroline would by then be five
years old, and Flaubert was keen that she should come too, for he
feared that his mother would otherwise spend the trip worrying
about her. In case the Hamard family objected, he urged his mother
to obtain a doctor's letter stating that the child needed to spend time
in a warm climate for the sake of her health. A similar subterfuge
was devised to thwart possible objections from Achille to Madame
Flaubert's departure: Du Camp sent her a prearranged letter saying
that Flaubert was ill and needed her in Italy. In the end, alternative
arrangements were made for Caroline, and in mid-April 1851 Madame
Flaubert, accompanied by a lady's maid, arrived in Rome, where she
found her younger son very much stouter and balder than before.

   Although Flaubert had initially found Rome disappointing, by
the time his mother arrived he had come to appreciate the city's
extraordinary artistic richness. Madame Flaubert, however, was soon
impatient to return home, and so mother and son left Rome on 8 May,
travelling by train via Pisa and Florence to Venice, where Flaubert
narrowly avoided arrest after losing his temper and punching a
customs official. The realization that his long period of freedom
and adventure was drawing to a close may well have contributed
to his ill temper. His mother, however, attributed it to the journey
itself. His behaviour had changed, she complained; he had become
'brutal'.[17] To avoid further difficulty, she cut short the Venetian visit,
and after brief stays in Milan and Paris, Flaubert and his mother
finally arrived home in Croisset on 16 June 1851. In readiness for
his return, Bouilhet and Du Camp had already unpacked the many
crates of articles Flaubert had acquired on the journey and sent
home in advance. His travels had lasted more than twenty months.

5

The *Madame Bovary* Years, 1851–7

PROSE. Easier to write than verse.

Gustave Flaubert, *Dictionary of Received Ideas*

As Flaubert and his mother were dining at home with friends a few days after their return to Croisset, an unexpected visitor called at the house and asked to see him. It was Louise Colet, with whom Flaubert had had no contact for nearly three years. Several weeks earlier, however, she had sent him a letter expressing disappointment that he had not come to bid her farewell in Paris before setting off for the Orient on a journey from which he 'might never return', and asking him to meet her in Paris for one last time on his way home.[1] On realizing that Flaubert had passed through Paris without contacting her, she had sent a second missive demanding the return of all her correspondence. It is unclear whether Flaubert ever received these letters, but he certainly did not respond, and when a furious Louise turned up at Croisset, she was not admitted to the house. Flaubert sent a note agreeing to meet her in town later that evening, but when she suggested they resume their liaison, he refused and advised her to marry Victor Cousin. His resolve soon weakened, however. A month later, he wrote to say he wished they could see one another calmly: 'I like your company when it is not *tempestuous*.'[2] By September 1851 their relationship had been rekindled.

Louise was not Flaubert's only preoccupation at this time, however. Not only was he busy writing up the notes from his Oriental journey, but ideas for the novel he had been mulling over on his travels had now crystallized to such an extent that he began to draw up preliminary plans, confident that he would soon be able to start writing. It appears to have been Louis Bouilhet who suggested that if Flaubert wished to set his new novel in the present, he might confect something around a recent local scandal involving the unhappy marriage of a young medical officer, Eugène Delamarre – a former student of Dr Flaubert's – and his second wife, Delphine. Wagging tongues in the Norman village of Ry alleged that Delphine had taken lovers and run up large debts before committing suicide, leaving a young daughter, who was orphaned when her father died not long after. Although Flaubert would later insist that all the characters in *Madame Bovary* were completely imaginary, and that the novel's setting – Yonville-l'Abbaye – was 'a place *that does not exist*', the story of Delphine Delamarre clearly provided him with a starting point.[3] In his memoirs, Du Camp makes the dramatic claim that it was when standing on a summit overlooking the rushing waters of the Nile's second cataract that Flaubert suddenly exclaimed: 'I've got it! *Eureka! Eureka!* I shall call her Emma Bovary,' though that version of events is somewhat undermined by the central character's name appearing as Marie rather than Emma in the novel's earliest plan.[4] What is not in dispute, however, is that on the evening of 19 September 1851, Flaubert finally began to compose *Madame Bovary*. He thought the novel would take about a year to complete.

Immediately, he became aware of problems. Determined not to produce 'Chateaubriandized Balzac' but to find his own, original voice, by the second day of writing he was already aware of stylistic difficulties that terrified him.[5] Before the week was up, however, he had to abandon work in order to accompany his mother and niece to London, where they were to stay with Jane Farmer, a former governess to his sister. The visit's main object was to find an English governess for little Caroline, now aged five and a half. Madame Flaubert duly selected Isabelle Hutton, a dark-haired young woman with a face scarred by smallpox. (Isabelle was an unfortunate choice, lasting less than a year at Croisset before being dismissed for ill-treating the little girl.) But Flaubert's first visit to London provided other distractions, including a foggy afternoon spent reminiscing with Henrietta Collier about their Trouville days. The family also visited the hugely popular Great Exhibition at the Crystal Palace, with Caroline perched on her uncle's shoulders, high above the milling crowds. Rather to his surprise, Flaubert was impressed by what he saw and took copious notes. Less to his taste was an excursion he and his mother made to Highgate Cemetery, where he was appalled by the ostentatious new tombs – travesties of Egyptian and Etruscan architecture surrounded by neatly raked flowerbeds. 'These people seem to have died in white gloves,' he reported to Louise.[6] The London visit would, however, leave traces in his novel – in the pharmacist Homais' overblown ideas for Emma Bovary's tomb ('a pyramid, or a temple of Vesta, a sort of rotunda') and in the depiction of Yonville's agricultural fair as a deflated parody of a great exhibition of modern industry, commerce, agriculture and fine arts.[7] Much later, a heavily pockmarked English governess would make a fleeting appearance in *Sentimental Education.*

Although he was soon back at work on *Madame Bovary*, Flaubert still had conflicting feelings about becoming a published author. Together with fellow writers Arsène Houssaye, Louis de Cormenin and Théophile Gautier, Maxime Du Camp had recently launched a new literary journal, the *Revue de Paris*, and had suggested that Flaubert contribute to it extracts from *The Temptation of St Anthony*. Bouilhet, however, advised Flaubert against publication, arguing that readers would find the work incomprehensible and that it would do him no favours. In a long, self-analytical letter, Flaubert poured out his uncertainties to Du Camp. If he published, he said, it would be for the stupidest of reasons: simply because he had been told to; he felt neither the need nor the desire to appear in print. Yet at the same time, he conceded that if he *were* to publish, it would have to be done properly. Knowing that he was temperamentally inclined to great surges of enthusiasm that quickly evaporated, he could not make a decision. 'If only you were aware of all the invisible webs of inactivity binding my body, and all the fog floating in my brain,' he complained to Du Camp: 'There are moments when I even think I'm wrong to want to write a sensible book instead of giving way to all the lyricism, violence and philosophico-fantastical eccentricities that occur to me.'[8] For Flaubert, art had always been a sufficient goal in itself – would it not be a debasement to seek publication? In his long and forthright reply, Du Camp did not hide his exasperation: Flaubert needed to make up his own mind about whether or not to publish, and he also needed to decide how to live his life; he was still tied to his mother's apron strings, isolating himself from the outside world; publication was not a necessity for him because he was fortunate enough to have a family who provided a generous financial cushion. Du Camp added, crushingly, 'you know how you live, but you don't know how other people do. You look around in vain and see only yourself, and in all your work you have only ever written about yourself.'[9]

For his part, Flaubert had grown increasingly irritated by Du Camp's drive and ambition, and by his willingness, in Flaubert's view, to compromise artistic ideals for the sake of commercial success. Those sentiments were compounded the following January when Du Camp was awarded the cross of the Legion of Honour. But Flaubert was also dissatisfied with his own behaviour. He felt alien and disaffected, characterizing himself to Louise as someone who had grown old (he was then 29) in all the excesses of solitude, highly strung to the point of collapse, tormented by suppressed passions, and filled with internal and external doubts.[10]

Soon, however, his personal discontent was overshadowed by convulsive events in France when, in the early hours of 2 December 1851, the President of the Republic, Louis-Napoléon Bonaparte, staged a coup d'état with the aim of prolonging his term of office. Martial law was declared, the National Assembly was dissolved, Louis-Napoléon's political opponents were arrested and over the next few days several hundred protestors and a number of innocent bystanders were killed by government troops. Staying in Paris at the time, Flaubert could hear the sound of cannon and gunfire from his rooms near the Tuileries and went down into the streets to observe events at close quarters. By his own account he narrowly missed being killed, but the violent spectacle exhilarated him: 'This time I wasn't cheated. It was terrific,' he reported to his uncle.[11] But he feared that France was about to enter a dark phase of history that somehow matched the mood of the people – a mixture of bitterness, rage and ennui.

For many of Flaubert's contemporaries, the coup d'état and Louis-Napoléon's proclamation of a Second Empire one year later marked a watershed. Writers who had been drawn into the political debate during the Revolution of 1848 turned away from political engagement in disgust, and their reluctance to involve themselves in political commentary was reinforced by the strict censorship laws soon imposed by the new imperial regime. As Charles Baudelaire famously put it, 'the 2nd of December *physically depoliticized* me.'[12] Victor Hugo, on the other hand, was vociferous in his opposition and fled the country to avoid arrest, eventually exiling himself in the Channel Islands from where he continued to publish scathing attacks on 'Napoléon le petit'. Knowing that the French authorities were likely to intercept Hugo's mail, Flaubert made elaborate arrangements for him to send his post to Jane Farmer in London for forwarding in an anonymous new envelope to Flaubert or Louise, but Hugo rarely used the ruse.

Flaubert's main reaction to the events, however, was to focus his energies on *Madame Bovary*. He wished not only to tell the story of a young woman who feels trapped in an unhappy marriage, but to present the life of a small Norman town as a microcosm of contemporary French society, which he saw as growing increasingly industrial, philistine and corrupt. Moreover, he wanted to achieve this without overt moralizing or explanation, believing that an author, like God in the universe, should always remain invisible in his work. 'The artist must manage to make posterity believe he never existed,' he explained to Louise.[13] Rather than tell his readers what to think, he aimed to let them see into the minds of his characters and present them with a reality viewed from multiple perspectives. Putting theory into practice proved to be a gruelling process, however.

Although the outline of *Madame Bovary*'s plot was in place, writing was painfully slow, and Flaubert soon realized that his estimate of completing the novel in a year was wildly optimistic. 'It's not going well. It's not working . . . You need superhuman willpower to write, and I am only a man,' he told Louise in April 1852.[14] A single page could take him a week or more; days could pass without a line. The plot was not his central concern, for the ideal to which he aspired was 'a book about nothing, a book with no external attachment', held together by the internal force of its style.[15] Although he claimed that the finest books were those with the least matter, he spent much time in detailed research, doubtless a welcome distraction from the blank page. He read books written for young girls, visited an agricultural fair, interrogated his brother about arsenic poisoning and the anatomy of club feet, consulted a lawyer for information on debts and promissory notes, and bombarded his antiquarian friend Alfred Baudry with queries about Rouen Cathedral. One afternoon was spent

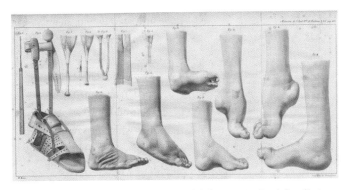

Fold-out illustration from a medical article on club feet, in *Mémoires de l'académie royale de médecine* (Paris, 1838), vol. VII.

viewing the countryside through pieces of differently coloured glass for a scene he would later delete, though the idea behind it – that the same thing may be perceived in many different ways – was important to his theme. As the writing progressed in fits and starts, Flaubert described the process as if it were a medical complaint: 'I'm scratching myself in torment. My novel finds it hard to get going. I have abscesses of style, and finding the right expression continuously makes me itch.'[16] Occasionally, he could write all night, but often he spent hours lying on his Turkish couch in what he described as 'a sort of imbecilic torpor, lacking the strength to make a gesture or have a thought'.[17]

In part, the difficulty lay in his subject-matter. Adopting the mindset and speech mannerisms of the inhabitants of a small, dull Norman town felt less congenial to Flaubert than the outlandish excesses of *The Temptation of St Anthony*: 'In *St Anthony*, I was at home. Now, I'm at the neighbour's place. I'm not at all comfortable there.'[18] It was painful to have to fill his mind with the banal dialogue of his mediocre characters. He persevered, however, often quoting the Comte de Buffon's famous remark about genius being merely a great aptitude for patience.

His niece would later describe him as 'harnessing himself to his work like an ox to the plough',[19] but his own self-images were equally dogged: he thought of himself as an old clock, stiff to wind up but able to keep ticking for a long time once started; as a horseman struggling to control a disobedient mount; as a stonemason, scraping excess mortar from meticulously placed building blocks; and as a boatbuilder painstakingly adjusting the planks of his hull. In practice, the scraping and adjusting involved a constant process of textual revision. It began with Flaubert reading the lines he had just written at the top of his voice, so that he could hear and modify the rhythm and cadence of his prose and detect any unwanted repetitions or stylistic deficiencies. His manuscript drafts are flecked with inky little underscorings to indicate words or individual letters that needed to be changed. But making corrections often created new difficulties, for his prose was so tightly woven that disturbing a single word could involve rewriting several pages. He added or pared down details, struck his pen through words or paragraphs, and recopied and reinstated earlier deletions, using a fresh sheet of paper for each new version. Afterthoughts spilled out into the margins. Passages often underwent many drafts, only to be eliminated.

One category of erasure is particularly revealing. Although Flaubert was determined to distance himself from the genre of Gothic horror that had been fashionable in his youth, he was unable to prevent gruesome images from bubbling to the surface of his imagination or returning to haunt him in nightmares. The manuscript drafts of *Madame Bovary* show the extent to which macabre elements kept forcing their way into his prose, only to be removed in the revision process. Deleted imagery includes pools of congealed blood, a sunken-eyed cadaver, dead animals, and references to drowning, flayed skin and decapitated or guillotined heads. The drafts also contain chilling echoes of the Hoffmann tales that had made such a terrifying impression on Flaubert as a child. After the laborious revision process, however, only minimal traces remained in the published version, though these troubling images continued to lurk in his mind.

In his revisions, Flaubert was greatly helped by Louis Bouilhet, who by this time had abandoned his medical studies in favour of literature and had become Flaubert's closest confidant. The two friends spent Sundays together at Croisset, reading and discussing each other's work and offering advice. Often, Bouilhet could quickly identify and solve a difficulty that had been troubling Flaubert, and when he moved to Paris in November 1853, Flaubert was distraught. Their Sunday sessions had become a regular habit over the years, and he dreaded the rupture as yet another painful loss: 'The only human ear I can talk to will no longer be there. That's something else gone, cast aside, destroyed for ever,' he lamented to Louise.[20] Flaubert and Bouilhet's intimate collaboration continued in letters and visits, however, and Bouilhet's intelligent and sympathetic assistance was such that Flaubert would later refer to him as his 'literary midwife'.[21]

Both men also spent much time reading and revising drafts of Louise Colet's work. Unlike Flaubert, Louise wrote easily and prolifically, and she had recently signed a contract for the publication of her collected works. Moreover, she was determined to win the prestigious poetry prize awarded annually by the Académie française, whose set theme that year was 'The Acropolis', a topic close to Flaubert's heart. He threw himself into the project, giving detailed advice, urging her to end the poem with a section on the barbarian invasion, and repeatedly admonishing her for writing too quickly and carelessly and at too great length. Louise's approach to composition was anathema to him, and she did not always welcome his and Bouilhet's revisions. Nerves became frayed: 'What is the point of asking our opinion and wearing us out if it's all going to end in wasted time and recriminations on both sides?' Flaubert complained. 'It's always

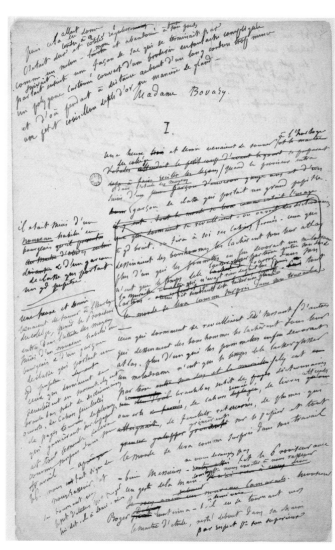

Early manuscript draft of the start of *Madame Bovary*; Brouillons, vol. 1, folio 3.

banalities that you defend – inanities that obscure your thought, disagreeable assonances and pedestrian turns of phrase.'[22]

Nevertheless, he continued to offer forthright commentaries on her work, and when the Académie awarded Louise the coveted prize in April 1854, Flaubert no doubt deserved some of the credit. By then, however, relations between the two had become increasingly strained. Annoyed that he often postponed promised visits in order to continue working on *Madame Bovary*, Louise accused him of being cold and unfeeling. Flaubert, for his part, was wearied by her hysterical accusations and neediness, and irritated by her dalliances with other men. (These included a flirtation with Alfred de Musset that had ended in injury when she escaped his drunken advances by leaping from a moving carriage.) Literary differences probably also played their part. Louise's work was too personal for Flaubert's taste, and furthermore, she had the high moral aim of changing mankind for the better, an aspiration that Flaubert considered utterly futile:

Why does the ocean move? What is *the aim* of nature? Well, I think humanity's aim is exactly the same. It is *because it is*, and you cannot do anything about it . . . We always turn in the same circle, we always roll the same rock![23]

The couple's final rift came suddenly. What caused it is unclear, though it was possibly triggered by Bouilhet's disclosure that Louise intended to become Flaubert's wife, despite the fact that soon after the pair met he had told her that nothing would ever persuade him to marry. What is certain is that on 6 March 1855 Flaubert sent Louise the following letter:

Madame,
I have learned that you took the trouble to come to see me three times yesterday evening. I was not at home. And for fear of the

rebuffs that such persistence might attract from me, good manners oblige me to inform you *that I shall never be at home*.[24]

It was their final communication.

Free from the emotional distraction of Louise, Flaubert returned to work with renewed vigour, confident that many women like Emma Bovary were suffering and weeping in villages across France. Although he almost certainly never uttered the famous words '*Madame Bovary, c'est moi*' that are often attributed to him, on the rare occasions when his writing flowed easily he would lose himself in his characters to the point of complete physical identification. As he described Emma's death, Flaubert tasted arsenic in his mouth and vomited. Emma and Rodolphe's love scene in the forest triggered an equally strong physical response:

> This has been one of the rare days in my life that I have completely spent in illusion from start to finish. Just now, at six o'clock, as I was writing the words *nervous attack*, I was so carried away, shouting so loudly and feeling so deeply what my little woman was feeling, that I was afraid I would have an attack myself. I rose from my desk and opened the window to calm down. My head was spinning.[25]

The manuscript reference to Emma's 'nervous attack', however, with its accompanying description of the physical symptoms of Flaubert's own nervous crises – cold feet, burning head, tight throat, racing heart, gasping breath – was deleted, like so many other details, before it could reach the published version.

By March 1856, the novel was complete. Flaubert read it over with Bouilhet one last time, and by the following month he was able to boast delightedly to a cousin that 'the year 1857 will sag beneath the weight of three volumes by your humble servant,' for he had sold *Madame Bovary* to Du Camp's *Revue de Paris*, and planned also to publish *The Temptation of St Anthony* and a medieval tale about St Julian the Hospitaller, for which he had already begun to read books on hunting.[26] All qualms about publishing his work had vanished. He now wanted to see himself in print as soon as possible, and his only concern was that Hugo's new collection of poetry, *Les Contemplations*, had just appeared and might steal his thunder. Flaubert's euphoria, however, was short-lived. Du Camp had doubts about the text of *Madame Bovary* and insisted on extensive cuts, but when a co-editor wanted even more to be removed, Flaubert refused to modify his text. The imminent publication of *Madame Bovary* by 'Faubert' had already been announced in the *Revue de Paris*, however, and in October 1856 the novel eventually began to appear in fortnightly instalments. Increasingly wary of the official censors, the *Revue*'s editors not only removed the account of Emma and Léon's erotically charged carriage ride from instalment five, but demanded yet more excisions. Again Flaubert stood his ground, refusing to change even a comma, so exasperated was he by the editors' apparent failure to understand the novel. 'You are attacking details, but you should be challenging the whole thing. The brutal element is deep within, not on the surface . . . A book's *blood* cannot be changed,' he told them.[27] His next step was to make an appointment to see the eminent lawyer Jules Senard.

When the next instalment appeared in early December, Flaubert discovered that the editors had made further cuts without his approval. Furious, he insisted that the final instalment be accompanied by a note denying his responsibility and telling readers that they had seen only fragments of the novel. Meanwhile, a Rouen journal that had been reprinting the *Revue de Paris*'s instalments grew alarmed on hearing of the dispute and stopped carrying them. Flaubert's decision to publish had turned into a nightmare; but worse was to come. Less than two weeks after the final instalment appeared, and just after signing an 800-franc contract with Michel Lévy to publish *Madame Bovary* in book form, Flaubert learned that he, his publisher and printer were to be prosecuted for 'outrage to morality and religion' and had been summoned to appear in court in a month's time.

Flaubert tried to put on a brave face, telling his friends that the prosecution was politically motivated, aimed not at his novel but at the troublesome *Revue de Paris*. To his brother, he boasted that the court case would bring him a week of fame, and that already 'all the society bitches are fighting over *Bovary*, trying to find obscenities that aren't there.'[28] Nevertheless, he was seriously worried: being charged with immorality was detrimental to a writer's reputation, and conviction could mean the end of his literary career. He feared not only that the fate of *Madame Bovary* was at stake, but that all novels were now endangered, along with the right to create them.

Flaubert spent January 1857 preparing his defence and trying to enlist support from influential contacts. Meanwhile, however, one unexpected response to the novel had given him great pleasure. Three days after publication of the final instalment, he received a message from a stranger in Angers who signed herself Marie-S. Leroyer de Chantepie. It was a rapturous letter of admiration from a reader, saying that in thirty years of avid novel-reading she had never been so deeply moved as by this 'masterpiece of naturalism and truth':

> Right from the start I recognized and loved [Emma Bovary] as a friend I might have known. I identified with her existence to such an extent that I felt as though she were both herself and me! No, this story is no fiction, it is true, this woman existed, and you must have witnessed her life, death and suffering . . . Oh sir, how did you come by this perfect understanding of human nature; it is a scalpel applied to the heart and soul; it is, alas, the world in all its hideousness.[29]

Caricature of Flaubert dissecting Madame Bovary, by A. Lemot. First published in *La Parodie* (5–12 December 1869).

So began an unlikely correspondence that lasted for almost twenty years. Although Flaubert would never meet this depressive, deeply religious and somewhat self-absorbed lady novelist, who had never left her provincial environment, writing to her became almost like communing with one of his own characters. 'Write whatever you like to me, often and at length,' he told her; 'I know you now and I love you.'[30] Her mysticism, her reclusiveness, her celibacy and her hysteria were all characteristics that intrigued Flaubert. They are traits shared by several of his characters, including St Anthony and Félicité in *A Simple Heart* (*Un coeur simple*, 1877), and to some extent by Flaubert himself. 'For long, Madame, I have lived your life,' he told Leroyer de Chantepie, acknowledging a real affinity with his unexpected correspondent.[31]

In January 1857, however, Flaubert's main focus was on the forthcoming trial. He scoured respected authors' works for passages that were more 'offensive' than anything in *Madame Bovary*, and pressed friends to lobby in high places on his behalf. There were some rays of hope: Empress Eugénie was rumoured to be on his side, the poet and former politician Alphonse de Lamartine was publicly supportive, and when a priest stabbed the Archbishop of Paris to death in early January, Flaubert saw it as a stroke of luck that would make *Madame Bovary*'s unflattering portrayal of the clergy pale into insignificance by comparison. But there were also long moments of despair when he imagined himself languishing in gaol.

The trial took place on 29 January. In a speech characterized by stupidity and bad faith, the prosecutor, Ernest Pinard, attacked the novel for failing to condemn adultery and for disparaging the Church. But Jules Senard demolished Pinard's position in a meticulous four-hour defence in which he argued that the novel was a literary masterpiece, a deeply moral work that depicted the dreadful consequences of adultery. By the time he came to address the allegedly scandalous description of Emma's last rites and pointed out that much of it came directly from the text of the Church's own Roman Ritual, it was clear that the case against Flaubert and the *Revue de Paris* would collapse. Their acquittal was formally announced on 7 February, and two months later, after the deadline for any possible judicial appeal had safely passed, *Madame Bovary* finally appeared in volume form, with a heartfelt dedication to Senard. Such was the publicity surrounding the trial that the novel soon had to be reprinted to satisfy demand from readers curious to see what all the fuss had been about. Flaubert, at the age of 35, suddenly found himself famous.

Eugène Giraud, *Gustave Flaubert*, *c.* 1856, oil on canvas.

6

The *Salammbô* Years, 1857–62

NOVELS. Pervert the masses. – Only historical novels
may be tolerated because they teach history.
Gustave Flaubert, *Dictionary of Received Ideas*

Although Flaubert was elated by the outcome of the trial and
its effect on sales of *Madame Bovary*, his initial euphoria soon
wore off, leaving him physically and emotionally exhausted and
wary of what was to come. Reviews had been mixed. 'There is
neither emotion, nor feeling, nor life in this novel,' wrote one
critic, whereas Louis de Cormenin hailed it as 'life itself'.[1] If
some reviewers welcomed Flaubert as an exciting new author
to watch, others complained of his 'puerile search for detail'
and compared his method to that of photography – soulless,
undiscriminating, recording whatever happened to fall within
his field of vision.[2] As he confided to Louise Pradier,

> All the uproar surrounding my first book seems so
> foreign to Art that it sickens and dazes me. How I miss
> the fishlike silence that I maintained until then. And
> I'm worried about the future: what could I write that
> would be more inoffensive than my poor *Bovary*?[3]

He was right to be cautious, for within a year the *Revue de Paris* had
been closed down by imperial decree. Although several extracts

from *The Temptation of St Anthony* had appeared – with judicious alterations – in *L'Artiste* just before his acquittal, he abandoned the idea of publishing the work in its entirety and shelved plans to write the tale of St Julian. In the aftermath of the *Madame Bovary* trial he felt tempted to retire into solitude and silence, publishing nothing and allowing himself to be forgotten, since free expression seemed impossible in the climate of Second Empire France.

Ceasing to write, however, was unthinkable for Flaubert. His solution was to avoid writing about contemporary French society and instead to plunge into a virtually unknown past, remote in both time and place. Telling Mademoiselle Leroyer de Chantepie in March 1857 that he felt sickened by the modern world into which he had 'dipped his pen too deeply', he announced that he was about to write a novel set in the third century BC.[4] The setting for the narrative that eventually became *Salammbô* would be Carthage in the aftermath of the First Punic War, and by the time he revealed his intentions to Leroyer de Chantepie, he had already begun the monumental task of researching the period. Friends were recruited to supply him with information about the ancient city's population, architecture, topography and flora, while he spent his days reading and making notes in Paris libraries before continuing the work at home late into the night.

The earliest plans for *Madame Bovary* had concentrated on thumbnail sketches of the novel's characters, with the plotline emerging from the interaction between their different personalities. With *Salammbô*, however, Flaubert tried a different approach. One of the earliest plans for the novel consists of a small sheet of blue paper, on one side of which is a short list of historical events, largely taken from Polybius' *Histories*. It notes how mercenaries engaged by Carthage turned against the city, and how their revolt spread to the surrounding areas and culminated in the long and terrible siege of Carthage before Hamilcar managed to free the city and annihilate the barbarian army. The other side of the sheet gives the briefest outline of the plot's fictional element: Hamilcar's daughter Salammbô (called Pyra at this early stage) and her attraction to the mercenaries; their theft of the sacred veil of the goddess Tanit; and the decision that Salammbô must retrieve the veil from the tent of the mercenaries' leader, Mâtho. A couple of words sketch the ending: 'Death of Mâtho – marriage – death of Pyra'. Flaubert's task was to combine the two outlines by weaving the invented tale of Salammbô and Mâtho into a historical setting, and by June he was satisfied that the plot's outline was in place.

In situating his new novel in a distant and forgotten civilization, Flaubert faced the practical problem of how to represent a culture and period of which almost no trace remained. He was acutely aware of the gaps in his knowledge of the period and went to great lengths to unearth all he could. For a description of a temple courtyard he read works on archaeology and a four-hundred-page memoir on the pyramidal cypress. He studied ancient warfare and the use of catapults and siege engines, and he spent a fortnight taking notes from the eighteen-volume Cahen Bible, with its extensive commentaries. 'I'm suffering from book indigestion,' he told a friend; 'I'm burping folios.'[5] Nevertheless, he continued to read, devouring a vast body of information from classical writers such as Pliny, Athenaeus, Plutarch and Xenophon, as well as from recent scholars, until, on 1 September 1857, he felt able to begin writing.

His niece Caroline and several close friends have left accounts of Flaubert at work in his large, book-lined study at Croisset with tall windows overlooking the garden and the Seine. They describe the objects that surrounded him – souvenirs of his travels, including arrows and amulets, an embalmed crocodile, the enormouse Turkish divan and a mummified foot which one of the servants had tried to clean with black boot polish, as well as the marble bust of his sister by Pradier and a watercolour of a young

Gertrude Collier. And they describe Flaubert himself, seated at his big table in a high-backed oak chair, enveloped in his customary brown robe, with his books and papers neatly ordered and his carefully sharpened goose-quill pens lying in readiness in a pewter dish. Bent over the desk, he would scribble feverishly for a few moments and then slump back in his seat with a despairing noise that sounded like a death rattle; or, if he felt he had found the right phrase, he would pace up and down the room repeating it at increasing volume, scanning its syllables and testing its sound and rhythm. His voice, hoarse from roaring out his sentences, needed jugfuls of water to ease it. As he agonized over the formidable task he had set himself with *Salammbô*, he frequently experienced what he referred to as 'the vertigo of the blank page', and his writing implements merged in his mind with images of drowning and bloodshed that had haunted him since his youth.[6] The quill pens bristling on his desk became fearsome, blood-letting spines and his inkwell seemed a black ocean that threatened to drown him.

Trying to find the right language to convey an ancient civilization caused Flaubert serious difficulty. He felt that he was veering between pomposity and platitude, and that his attempts to express moments of violent intensity merely sounded melodramatic. French often lacked the precise word he needed, forcing him to resort to circumlocutions, which 'diluted the local colour like a sauce'.[7] Allied to this were problems with the psychological element. Whereas he had been able to immerse himself in *Madame Bovary*'s characters, whose mentality he understood only too well, giving a convincing account of ancient Carthage seemed impossible because a sense of its inhabitants' innermost feelings eluded him. 'I *feel* that it's false', he told Mademoiselle Leroyer de Chantepie,

> and that my characters cannot have talked like that . . . I can glimpse the truth, but it does not penetrate me, the emotional side is lacking . . . If everything I write is empty and flat,

it is because I do not throb with my heroes' emotions.
It's as simple as that.[8]

In January 1858, recovering from influenza and still wrestling
with the early stages of *Salammbô*, Flaubert decided that the
only solution was to travel to North Africa, visit Carthage and
its surroundings, and experience for himself the last remnants
of the civilization he struggled to evoke. Historians whom he
admired, such as Edgar Quinet and Victor Cousin, had stressed
the importance of visiting historical sites, arguing that the spirit
of an age left traces on its physical surroundings, and no doubt
their thinking influenced Flaubert's decision. The appeal of
escaping for nearly two months to a sun-baked 'land of dates'
must also have contributed, however, for the period leading up
to his departure had been particularly trying.[9] His mother had
been seriously ill with pleurisy, and fever had incapacitated his
valet, Narcisse; both caused Flaubert great alarm. There had also
been tiresome family duties relating to the forthcoming marriage
of his niece Juliette, Achille's daughter. Moreover, a temptingly
lucrative proposal for a theatrical adaptation of *Madame Bovary*
had ended in disappointment and recrimination when it emerged
that he would have been allowed no involvement in the script.
During the same period, Paris was shaken when three bombs
were thrown at the Emperor and Empress's carriage as it arrived
at the Opéra, in an unsuccessful assassination attempt that left
eight dead and over 150 injured. The government's reaction, which
included deporting many of Napoléon III's political opponents to
Algeria and closing down journals hostile to the regime, added
to the sense of discontent, and by mid-April Flaubert was only
too glad to leave everything behind and set off on his travels,
with six copies of *Madame Bovary* stowed in his luggage.

He disembarked at Stora in northern Algeria on 18 April,
having gone on deck at five that morning to gaze across the dark

Georges Rochegrosse, *Flaubert's Study at Croisset*, 1874, watercolour.

sea towards the African coast. From there, his journey took him inland to the ancient city of Constantine, through landscape that reminded him of central France but where Barbary lions roamed, and from there he continued towards Tunis. As always, he took notes, but this time, even jotting down his impressions felt like hard work. Apologizing to Bouilhet for sending him a boring letter, he explained:

> I have neither the time nor strength to send you descriptions
> – I am so exhausted in the evenings that I can barely make
> a few notes. I don't think about my novel at all. I look at the
> countryside, that is all, and am enjoying myself enormously.[10]

Nevertheless, his travel notes record details of every kind, from the rowdy, malodorous Europeans who shared his coach, to the grey-white robes and brown faces of locals crowding round an old snake charmer, and include random snippets such as, 'the silk worm sleeps with its head raised.'[11] They reveal his attempts to capture unfamiliar sense impressions, as he notes the 'smell of tobacco, coffee, musk and above all of benzoin' or describes 'cafés full of people and sound, with music screeching and buzzing and voices yelping above it'; and they show his delight in casually observed details – the tranquil silhouette of a palm tree against a moonlit sky, or the way that horses' legs cast long, thin shadows on the desert sand, making them look like giraffes.[12]

Travelling without a companion meant that Flaubert was free to investigate what interested him for as long as he liked. He was especially interested in any remains from the period in which his novel was set, but the ancient ruins he saw in Utica, La Marsa and Carthage were not easy to decipher: 'it is difficult to tell rocks from ruins at a distance,' he noted. Even from close up, 'shapeless ruins, great blocks of masonry looking as if an earthquake had overturned them' were hard to interpret.[13] Their unknowability intrigued him: 'Is this a pier or the remains of a square tower?' he wondered; 'were these walls?'[14] He paid close attention to ancient cisterns and aqueducts, noting how they related to the surrounding landscape and how the changing light affected their appearance. But much remained mysterious, and something of this impenetrability would eventually permeate *Salammbô*, affecting not only buildings and ruins but emotions, gestures and beliefs.

With transport costs, guides and bearers to be paid, however, travel proved expensive. The Flaubert family's finances were less healthy than they had once been: income from their land and properties had fallen, and Madame Flaubert had recently had to sell her carriage and dispense with an English tutor for Caroline. Reluctantly, then, Flaubert left the pink sunsets of North Africa behind and sailed for Marseilles on 2 June. Arriving home in Croisset six days later after a short stay in Paris, he felt exhausted and disoriented. 'I have spent the last three days doing almost nothing but sleep,' he noted at the end of his travel journal; 'I feel as if I have emerged from two months at a masked ball.'[15]

Soon, however, he plunged back into *Salammbô*. Steeped in the sights, sounds and smells of the Orient, fascinated by the people he had met and by the archaeological remains he had seen at first hand, he at last felt able to write about Carthage with truth and conviction. Everything he had already completed was discarded. '*Carthage* has to be completely redone – or rather, done,' he told Ernest Feydeau on 20 June. '*I'm demolishing all of it*. It was ridiculous! Impossible! False!'[16] His new-found confidence that visiting North Africa had enabled him to find the right tone was short-lived, however. No one had ever undertaken a work that presented such problems of language and style, he complained. Using circumlocutions would dilute the effect he sought; writing in conventional French would sound banal; and he was determined not to imitate the elevated historical style of writers such as Fénelon or Chateaubriand. By October he was in despair about the project, and once more his health suffered. Complaining of stomach pains and of an aching head and limbs, he took to his bed. The problem was psychological as much as physical. 'I have *the black sickness*,' he confided to Feydeau. 'I had it before for eighteen months when I was young and strong, and it nearly killed me.'[17]

In due course, however, the novel began to progress more easily, much helped by the departure of Madame Flaubert and Caroline to spend the winter in Paris. Flaubert could now settle into a routine of his own, rising at midday and writing deep into the night, meeting no one, rarely seeing daylight and losing track of what day of the week it was. Despite the presumable presence of servants, he felt he was living in a 'complete, objective void', and he loved it, as he told Feydeau at the beginning of December:

> I have been completely alone for eight days now . . .
> Solitude intoxicates me like alcohol. I'm insanely cheerful
> for no real reason, and I bellow all through the house, on
> my own, shouting loud enough to burst my lungs.[18]

He found ways around the language problem that had bothered him, introducing esoteric vocabulary to create the sense of a period far distant in time and place, and communicating the strangeness of his characters' language by means of suggestion. By reducing direct speech to a minimum, by employing unfamiliar names such as Schahabarim and Narr'Havas, and by making liberal use of the un-Gallic letter K (for example, Kabyres, Kapouras, Khamon, Kinisdo, Melkarth), he subtly conveyed the sounds of an outlandish tongue. The novel's overall colour and tone were more important than details of character or plot, he decided, and in *Salammbô* he wanted 'to do something purple'.[19]

Since this novel was set during the Mercenary Wars, there was no need for Flaubert to suppress gruesome images of bloodshed and dismemberment, as he had repeatedly struggled to do while working on the drafts of *Madame Bovary*. On the contrary, his new subject offered endless scope for purging some of the private horrors that tormented him. He could pour them into descriptions of cataclysmic violence, such as Hamilcar's war elephants eviscerating barbarian soldiers and charging onwards with entrails dangling from their tusks, or the great piles of corpses, most of them lacking faces or arms, that remained in the Defile of the Axe after the annihilation of the mercenary army. 'I am killing men like flies. I am spilling torrents of blood,' he reported with satisfaction.[20] Once again he consulted medical textbooks, as well as first-person accounts of extreme dehydration and starvation written by survivors from the raft of the *Medusa*. As with *Madame Bovary*, Flaubert identified closely and physically with his characters' suffering. Writing about the siege of Carthage left him physically exhausted and with muscles aching, but he took a strange pride in sending friends amplified accounts of his bodily exertions:

> You cannot imagine what a burden it is to carry all this mass
> of decaying carcasses and horrors . . . The poisoning of
> La Bovary made me vomit into my chamber pot. The

assault on Carthage is making my arms hurt . . . *I can't
go on*. The siege of Carthage which I am just finishing
has done for me. I'm sweating blood, pissing boiling
oil, shitting catapults and burping out projectiles.[21]

Although Flaubert had relished the thought of leaving behind
the modern world of *Madame Bovary*, and freeing himself from petit
bourgeois characters and their banal exchanges, the manuscript
notes and drafts for *Salammbô* reveal that he was recreating an
ancient world that also bore traces of contemporary France. One
jotting reads, 'Salammbô had become bourgeoise'; another refers
to the 'political clubs of Carthage'.[22] Moreover, although the
aqueduct that plays a central role in the novel was, by Flaubert's
own admission, an anachronism, the writing of *Salammbô* coincided
with the controversial construction of an aqueduct to bring fresh
water into Second Empire Paris. Social divisions, tensions between
Church and state, France's colonial policy in North Africa, reform
banquets, bourgeois manners and elements of Haussmann's redesign
of the capital all find echoes in the novel, though in the final version
Flaubert was careful merely to hint at the presence of contemporary
parallels. Tellingly, he informed friends that he had chosen Carthage
as his setting because it was the most corrupt civilization in the world,
and he took defiant delight in imagining the public's reaction:

Yes, people will give me hell, you can count on that.
Salammbô will 1. annoy the bourgeoisie, that is to say
everyone; 2. disgust the nerves and soul of the sensitive;
3. irritate archaeologists; 4. seem incomprehensible to ladies;
5. make me out to be a pederast and a cannibal. Let's hope so![23]

Although Flaubert needed isolation in order to write, by nature
he was highly sociable, and his new fame had brought him new
literary friends. During his stays in Paris he frequented the celebrated

salon of the *demi-mondaine* Madame Sabatier, where he met many
of the leading writers and artists of the day. He was now part of
a wide literary circle that included Ernest Feydeau, Théophile
Gautier, Edmond and Jules de Goncourt, and Charles Baudelaire
(whose *Les Fleurs du mal*, inspired in part by Madame Sabatier,
had been deemed an 'outrage to public morality' when he stood
trial shortly after the unsuccessful prosecution of *Madame Bovary*).
The Goncourt brothers, who documented their own wide literary
acquaintanceship in their waspish and gossip-filled *Journal*, described
many of their encounters with Flaubert. Their impressions were
not always favourable, as the entry for 16 March 1860 makes clear:

> There is something provincial and affected about him.
> One has the vague feeling that he went on all those travels
> partly to amaze the inhabitants of Rouen. His mind is
> as heavy and fat as his body . . . There are very few ideas
> in his conversation and they are presented loudly and
> solemnly . . . He is clumsy, excessive and without lightness
> in anything . . . His bovine cheerfulness lacks charm.[24]

Nevertheless, Flaubert confided in them, shared with them his
enthusiasms and aversions, introduced them to doctors who could
provide medical information for their next novel, *Soeur Philomène*,
and treated them, in March 1861, to a sonorously dramatic reading
of the opening chapter of *Salammbô*. It was, they noted with some
surprise, an astonishing and ingenious feat of the imagination.

Flaubert's most supportive critic, however, was still Louis
Bouilhet, who continued – either by letter or during visits to
Croisset – to read, discuss and correct Flaubert's drafts and to
advise him on aspects of plot. The collaboration worked both
ways, for Flaubert took an equally close interest in Bouilhet's
poems and plays, even assuming the role of negotiator when
it came to finding a Paris theatre willing to stage them. By the

Louis Bouilhet photographed by Étienne Carjat, 1864.

summer of 1861 Flaubert had started work on 'Moloch', the eighth chapter of *Salammbô*, but despite Bouilhet's encouragement and with the novel's end almost in sight, his doubts multiplied. He feared the overall plan was defective, but it was too late to change it. He worried, too, that the endless battle scenes would bore his readers, that everything about the novel would infuriate them; already he could imagine the stupid comments it would attract. As he continued to torment himself, friends feared for his sanity. But despite his complaints and protestations, he persevered, and on Easter Sunday, 20 April 1862, at seven o'clock in the morning, he finally finished *Salammbô*. '*I cannot take any more,*' he wrote to Mademoiselle Leroyer de Chantepie.[25]

Earlier that month, the first part of Hugo's *Les Misérables* had appeared in print, and as with *Madame Bovary*, Flaubert was concerned lest a new work by the great '*père* Hugo' overshadow the publication of his own novel. *Salammbô* still required final revisions and corrections, and a contract with the publisher Michel Lévy was yet to be negotiated with the help of his lawyer, Ernest Duplan. He gave Duplan strict instructions: Lévy was not to read the manuscript in advance; under no circumstances was the novel to have illustrations; Lévy should know that Flaubert had promised a friend of a friend that she could translate the novel into German and had agreed that Ernest Reyer could write a *Salammbô* opera; and he wanted to be paid a lump sum rather than a royalty for each copy sold, since he did not trust sales figures. Lévy agreed. He offered to pay Flaubert 10,000 francs, though this was to be kept secret, for he intended to whip up excitement by telling the press he had bought the novel for three times that sum. When the time came, Flaubert paid meticulous attention to the printing. He insisted that there should be no more than thirty lines per page ('My style is cramped enough without making things even more difficult for the reader'), that each new chapter should start on a recto ('The eye is naturally drawn there. The beginnings of my chapters are worthy of a fine page') and that the circumflex accent on Salammbô must be more shapely. Nothing was less Phoenician than a narrow circumflex, he told Lévy.[26]

When *Salammbô* finally appeared to great fanfare in December 1862, reviewers were bewildered. A second novel from the author of *Madame Bovary* had been widely advertised and eagerly awaited, but instead of a sequel, readers found themselves confronted with a work that seemed to fit no recognizable category. 'What is *Salammbô*?' asked *La Gazette de France*. 'To pose the question is already to put the book on trial.'[27] Reviewers described it variously as an epic, a prose poem, a drama, an archaeological tour de force and a guide book to Carthage: the work seemed impossible to pigeonhole. The response indicates how far Flaubert had diverged from what his contemporaries expected of a historical novel, and most critics disapproved. 'It would be impossible to go to greater efforts to be so prodigiously boring,' sniffed *Le Monde*, while *Le Figaro*'s appraisal was so hostile that Madame Flaubert feared her son might challenge its author to a duel.[28] (Rightly or wrongly, Flaubert suspected that particular review to have been prompted by Louise Colet.) On the other hand, when the eminent critic Charles Augustin Sainte-Beuve devoted three substantial articles to a detailed assessment of the novel, Flaubert was delighted that a writer he admired had taken his work so seriously. Defending his aims in an open letter to Sainte-Beuve, Flaubert explained that he had 'wanted to fix a mirage by applying the procedures of the modern novel to Antiquity', and had 'tried to be simple'.[29] He was also cheered to learn that he had earned 'the HHHHATRED OF PRIESTS', for the author of *Salammbô* had been denounced from church pulpits, accused of inventing obscene costumes and encouraging paganism.[30] The one criticism that infuriated him, however, came from the Louvre archaeologist Guillaume Froehner, who wrote a vehement attack alleging that *Salammbô* was full of factual errors. Stung into publishing a detailed and crushing rebuttal, Flaubert revealed the astonishing extent of his research as he exposed his adversary's ignorance of the history and culture of ancient Carthage.

Although reviews of *Salammbô* were generally cool, the novel was enthusiastically received by a reading public mesmerized by its exotic beauty. 'I wrote a book for a very limited number of readers,' Flaubert commented to Le Poittevin's sister, Laure, 'and it turns out that the public are latching onto it. Blessed be the god of the bookshop!'[31] The work generated such excitement that the Paris Opéra explored the possibility of a *Salammbô* opera with music by Verdi, the Palais-Royal theatre staged a popular pastiche entitled *Folammbô, or, Carthaginian Capers*, and a *Salammbô* pastry was invented in the novel's honour. Suddenly, Flaubert found new doors opening. He was welcomed into the elite literary salon of Napoléon III's cousin, Princess Mathilde, while her brother, Prince Napoléon, offered him friendly invitations to the Palais-Royal and to the imperial box at the opera. ('Ah, how far removed all this is from our dear little provincial life,' Flaubert commented self-mockingly to his niece.[32]) Among the book's new admirers were the composer Hector Berlioz, who approached Flaubert for expert advice on Carthaginian costumes for the staging of his new opera, *The Trojans*, and the novelists George Sand and Ivan Turgenev, whose appreciation of *Salammbô* marked the beginning of long and important friendships with Flaubert.

For a brief moment, however, the response that most excited him was that of Empress Eugénie, who personally asked him for details of Salammbô's costume, which she wished to have copied for a fancy dress ball. He immediately set about commissioning illustrations, only to cancel on learning that the empress had decided that a Salammbô dress would be inappropriately revealing. Other society ladies were less reticent, however, and exotic, diaphanous Salammbô outfits briefly became all the rage. Madame Rimsky-Korsakov caused a sensation by appearing at Count Walewski's ball with her hair flowing loose beneath an elaborate headdress and

Drawing of Salammbô by Henri Valentin, published in *L'Illustrateur des dames* (22 February 1863).

wearing a snake-encrusted Salammbô gown designed by Charles Frederick Worth. Two years after the novel's publication, Maxime Du Camp sent Flaubert a photograph of the Queen of Spain in a Salammbô costume. 'She received compliments on its accuracy,' he told his friend; 'It's pretty daring, and I thought it would amuse you to have this piece of filth.'[33] Whether Flaubert was amused or not, it was further confirmation that, in a very different way from *Madame Bovary*, *Salammbô*, too, had made its mark.

7

The *Sentimental Education* Years, 1862–9

ARTS. Are quite useless, since they are being replaced
by machines which make things better and faster.

Gustave Flaubert, *Dictionary of Received Ideas*

As soon as the end of *Salammbô* was in sight, Flaubert began
to turn his mind to his next project. He toyed with several
possibilities, but the one that most attracted him could hardly
have been further removed from the world of ancient Carthage.
Doubtless that was part of its appeal, but so too was the fact
that the unlikely scheme was a collaborative venture with Louis
Bouilhet and their mutual friend Charles d'Osmoy. The plan was
for the three men to co-write a *féerie* – a pantomime-like fantasy
play with music and spectacular stage effects – a genre hugely
popular in France since the beginning of the century. Flaubert
was excited at the prospect of indulging his old love of the theatre
once again. In July 1862 he told the Goncourt brothers that he
had just read 33 *féeries* at a stretch, and the following month he
read many more in a stiflingly hot Vichy while accompanying his
mother and Caroline on a health cure. But he found the plays dull
and silly, and wanted his *féerie* to be different – bold, passionate
and unconventional. Du Camp urged him on, telling him it
would do him good to write something quickly for a change.

Work on *The Castle of Hearts* (*Le Château des coeurs*) began
in earnest in the summer of 1863, but Flaubert's collaborators

were less enthusiastic about modernizing the genre, and when the three friends congregated in Croisset that August, the piece they put together was a satirical extravaganza involving fairies, giants, bankers, lovers, grocers and bureaucrats in a surreal world where the hearts of men have been stolen by gnomes and locked away in a castle. When Flaubert read the script aloud to the Goncourts in October, they were stunned that a novelist whose writing they greatly admired could have produced a work of such vulgarity. Theatre after theatre turned the play down, and although Flaubert remained convinced of its merit and tried for many years to persuade theatre managers to stage it, *The Castle of Hearts* was not performed in his lifetime.

While still labouring over *Salammbô*'s proof corrections in Paris in the autumn of 1862, however, Flaubert contemplated other projects. He felt a pressing need to write, and the following spring saw him working simultaneously on plans for two new novels, uncertain which to develop. He was confident that the plan for one of them, the embryonic *Bouvard and Pécuchet* (*Bouvard et Pécuchet*), was sound, but he knew it might land him in trouble: 'I shall be hounded out of France and Europe if I write that book,' he told Jules Duplan.[1] Of the other project he was less sure. It was for 'a modern Parisian novel', but he feared the plot he had in mind was structurally defective – it refused 'to make a pyramid', as he put it. Nevertheless, possibly on Bouilhet's advice, this was the project he decided to pursue. He tried to explain his aims and misgivings to Mademoiselle Leroyer de Chantepie:

> I want to write the moral history of the men of my generation;
> 'sentimental' would be more accurate. It is a book about
> love and passion, but passion such as can exist nowadays –
> inactive, in other words. As I have conceived it, the subject is
> profoundly true, I think, but probably not very entertaining
> for that very reason. It's rather lacking in facts and drama;

and then the action is stretched over too great a length of time. I am having a lot of difficulty and am full of anxiety.[2]

As he began work on the novel to which he would eventually give the same title as his unpublished first novel – *Sentimental Education* – Flaubert was in poor health. That autumn he took to his bed for a week, suffering from clusters of painful boils which he feared might develop into anthrax. Two weeks later he was again bedridden, unable to move because of rheumatic pains and tormented by intense itching. Over the next months, he continued to complain of boils, pain and insomnia. In fact, painful boils plagued Flaubert for most of his life, often causing him to cancel social engagements or confining him to bed. Even when well, by this stage in his life (he turned 41 that December) he was disinclined to physical activity. Reluctant even to venture out into the garden unless nagged by his mother, he preferred to remain indoors all day, working and smoking, and sitting so still that the sight of his motionless form sometimes alarmed Madame Flaubert.

Although he still had 'mad urges to go off to China or the Indies', real escape of that kind was no longer possible.[3] In May 1863, however, claiming that he could no longer stand Normandy's lush spring greenery, he left Croisset for his regular apartment at 42 boulevard du Temple in Paris, continuing a pattern of alternating between the provinces and the capital that had by then become habitual – a pattern Frédéric Moreau echoes in *Sentimental Education* as he shuttles restlessly between Nogent-sur-Seine and Paris. In the capital, Flaubert led a gregarious life. His letters home to Caroline brim with gossip about visits or dinners with friends, including those he met in Magny's restaurant at the lively fortnightly reunions of writers and artists that Sainte-Beuve and the illustrator Paul Gavarni had initiated in November 1862. There, Flaubert was likely also to find Louis Bouilhet, Théophile Gautier, the Goncourt brothers, Ernest

Renan and Hippolyte Taine, and engage in the type of heated debates about life and literature he so missed in Normandy.

When in Paris, however, Flaubert worried about how his mother was coping in Croisset. 'Take good care of her, my dear Caro,' he wrote to his niece in December 1863; 'see to it that she doesn't notice my absence too much.'[4] But he was also concerned about Caroline. By then nearly eighteen, she was of marriageable age and had fallen deeply in love with her drawing teacher, Joanny Maisiat, a forty-year-old painter of some distinction. Maisiat was an attentive tutor to his gifted pupil, introducing her to great works of art in the Louvre and taking her on expeditions around Croisset to draw closely observed scenes from nature. He was a good friend of Flaubert's, and it was to Maisiat that Flaubert turned when he needed details about painting for *Sentimental Education* – but the prospect of Caroline marrying an impoverished artist horrified the Flaubert family. Instead, they urged her to accept a proposal from Ernest Commanville, a timber merchant eight years her senior who owned a sawmill in Dieppe. Caroline wept and resisted. In Paris, Flaubert followed the painful process from a distance, and although his letters to Caroline were loving and sympathetic, there was no doubt where his preference lay:

> Human life feeds on more than poetic ideas and exalted feelings . . . Well, the thought of my poor niece married to an impoverished man is so appalling that I do not entertain it for a moment. Yes, my darling, I declare that I would rather see you marry a millionaire grocer than a great man with no money.[5]

It was an astonishing reaction from someone so disparaging of bourgeois businessmen, someone for whom art was the highest value and 'grocer' a scornful term of abuse. But both Flaubert and his niece had been brought up in financial comfort, which he knew was as important to her as it was to him. Around

New Year's Day Caroline finally relented and agreed to marry the prosperous timber merchant; many years later, she would say it felt as if she had been cast out of Parnassus. A relieved Madame Flaubert wrote to her lawyer asking him to inform Émile Hamard of his daughter's impending marriage, and, if possible, prevent him from attending the wedding. In early April 1864 the couple married – without the bride's father in attendance – and immediately left for a honeymoon in Italy. Mindful of the ill-fated Italian honeymoon of Caroline's mother, Madame Flaubert suffered agonies of anxiety during her niece's absence, imagining accidents or illness if letters failed to arrive regularly from Italy. She and Flaubert were reassured, however, to receive one with a postscript indicating that Caroline was very pleased with her new husband.

Caroline Commanville, Flaubert's niece, photographed *c.* 1865.

The difficulties over establishing his niece's emotional future had disrupted Flaubert's work on the novel, but soon he returned to planning his hero's own emotional and sexual development, from a timid boyhood encounter with the local prostitute, through his unsatisfactory entanglements with four different women, to the wry reminiscences of maturity. In describing Frédéric Moreau's sentimental education, Flaubert aimed not only to narrate the emotional progress of one individual, but to chart the mentality of his contemporaries as they lived through a recent and climactic period of French history, which he knew would be as familiar to his readers as *Salammbô*'s mercenary wars had been foreign. His research therefore had to be meticulous, particularly since he had spent the tumultuous June days of the Revolution of 1848 in hiding with Caroline and his mother, concerned less by current events than by the need to keep his little niece safe from her father. He passed long hours in Paris libraries reading newspaper reports and works by social and political thinkers, he consulted friends, and in August he travelled along the Seine from Paris through Villeneuve-saint-Georges, Corbeil, Melun and Montereau to Sens, needing to see for himself places he wished to mention in the novel. Then, on 1 September 1864, he at last began to write.

The first chapter he found particularly difficult – the consequence, he believed, of having spent too long without writing – but Bouilhet reassured him that the novel's plan now had the overall coherence to become a fine book. Nevertheless, Flaubert's old self-doubt remained. If representing the vanished civilization of Carthage in *Salammbô* had posed problems, he soon realized that writing about the recent past presented real difficulties of its own. As he told his old friend Jules Duplan,

I am having a lot of trouble fitting my characters into the political events of '48! I'm afraid that the background will overwhelm the foreground. That is the problem

with historical novels. Characters from history are more
interesting than fictional ones, especially when the
passions of the latter are not very intense . . . *It's hard!*[6]

Moreover, the Paris of the 1840s, whose topography was so
important to his narrative, was very different from the Paris that
Flaubert saw around him in the 1860s, for in the intervening
period many crowded areas of the city had been demolished
under Baron Haussmann's direction to make way for new streets
and boulevards and public monuments. Familiar landmarks
vanished, and even native Parisians needed to consult new
maps to find their way around. Flaubert turned the changing
city to his advantage, however, so that in the novel, that sense of
temporal and physical disorientation finds a counterpart in the
confusion and uncertainty surrounding the Revolution of 1848.

The distractions of his new Parisian life as a famous author
made it hard for Flaubert to settle down to writing. That
November, for example, he received an invitation to one of the
Emperor's famous *séries* at Compiègne, spending seven days at
the imperial palace in the company of the royal family, courtiers
and a hundred or so other distinguished guests. Rather too late,
he realized that the visit coincided with the Empress's birthday,
when guests were expected to offer her flowers. He sent an urgent
message to Jules Duplan, asking him to arrange without fail
for a huge bouquet of white camellias to be delivered. 'I want it
to be extra chic,' Flaubert told him, 'You have to make a good
impression if you belong to the lower orders.'[7] He had expected to
spend the week in boredom, but despite the strictly programmed
activities and the multiple changes of costume demanded by
protocol, he was surprised to find himself taking great pleasure
in the stay. He also much enjoyed Prince Napoléon's grand ball
at the Palais-Royal a few months later, where he was pleased to
discover that about two hundred of the guests were already known

to him. With some glee, he reported to Caroline that he had seen the legendary Regent Diamond sparkling in the Empress's crown, and had sat next to a princess '*on the steps of the throne*'.[8]

A further distraction from writing was the state of his finances. Flaubert had extravagant tastes and never found it easy to economize, and moving in such elevated circles required considerable outlay, as did the rental of his apartment in the boulevard du Temple and the refurbishments he had ordered for his Croisset study. Faced with repeated requests for money, his mother grew increasingly concerned: if Flaubert had so overspent his allowance in a year when he had mainly lived expense-free in Croisset, how would he manage in the future? Moreover, how would she herself manage if she had to continue to fund his extravagant lifestyle? In desperation, she wrote to her lawyer in February 1865, begging him to verify her son's debts (which she suspected him of exaggerating) and persuade him to rein in his expenditure. Flaubert in turn sent a somewhat testy letter to the lawyer, giving his side of the argument and providing evidence of long-overdue bills, which included 2,728 francs to his decorator, 1,883 francs to his tailor and 498 francs to his glover:

> Nothing is more *painful* to me than continually asking my mother for money. Try to persuade her that I do not go in for mad debauchery! . . . And since she has decided to pay my debts, let her do her good deed *well*, without too much recrimination.[9]

To settle her son's debts Madame Flaubert had to sell a family property, and in May Flaubert reluctantly abandoned Paris and its expensive diversions for Croisset, telling Jules Duplan he was retreating into his hole to work.

In Croisset, however, the days dragged, and as usual he found writing arduous. Overwhelmed by gloomy memories and dark thoughts, he sank deeper into a despondency he once likened to a surging black tide that threatened to drown him. He needed to escape. Little more than a month after leaving Paris, he was back in the capital, and in late June he travelled to London, this time on his own. Waiting for him at Victoria station was Juliet Herbert, who had been Caroline's governess while he was writing *Madame Bovary* and to whom he had been very close. The two had translated Byron's poem 'The Prisoner of Chillon' together, and had spent long evenings by the fireside in his Croisset study working on an English translation of *Madame Bovary*. The exact nature of his relationship with Juliet has been the subject of much speculation, but she was clearly held in great affection by all the Flaubert family and had visited them several times since leaving their employment. Flaubert stayed in London for two and a half weeks that summer, visiting most of the main tourist sites – the British Museum, London Zoo, the National Gallery, Hyde Park, Kew Gardens, Hampton Court Palace, the Palace of Westminster, Kensington Gardens and the Crystal Palace, which he had seen on his first London visit in 1851, now on its new site in Sydenham. He also rode the excitingly new underground railway and paid another visit to Jane Farmer in Hornsey. *Sentimental Education* was never far from his mind, however, for shortly before leaving London, he wrote to Caroline that he had seen 'many very curious things, and several that will be very useful for my novel', although few traces of his English experience are visible in the finished text.[10]

After London, Flaubert was not yet ready to return to his desk. Changing trains in Paris, he travelled on to Baden Baden to spend a week with Maxime Du Camp and his mistress, Adèle Husson, a visit during which the two men discussed the progress of Flaubert's novel. Du Camp would later claim that in portraying Frédéric as hesitant and timid, wary of female commitment, and liable to make resolutions that evaporated whenever action was called for, Flaubert had unconsciously portrayed himself. At the time, however, the two men would certainly have talked of Élisa Schlésinger, on whom the character of Madame Arnoux is loosely based, for both knew that she had been committed to a mental hospital suffering from severe depression, and Du Camp had recently seen her in Baden Baden looking thin and wild-eyed, her once dark hair turned completely white.

On his return to Croisset towards the end of July, Flaubert found his mother in a pitiful state, in great pain from an attack of shingles. He worried that she might be dangerously ill – 'everything is serious at the age of seventy-two,' he told friends.[11] But he had been home for only three days when concern for his mother was suddenly eclipsed by a shocking and unforeseen event that devastated all the Flaubert family. On 29 July 1865, Adolphe Roquigny, the 34-year-old husband of Flaubert's niece Juliette, committed suicide by shooting himself in the head at home in Ouville, near Dieppe, while Juliette and their two young children were in the next room. On hearing the news, Flaubert immediately left Croisset for Ouville and spent the next two days amid the wails and tears of Juliette's grief-stricken household. He had been fond of Roquigny, a gentle soul, and the death seemed incomprehensible – 'sudden madness' was the only explanation Flaubert could offer.

Emotionally exhausted, he returned to Croisset, where his mother's condition was causing her such agony that Flaubert slept in his study to avoid being kept awake by her cries. Her doctor treated her with vesicatories and recommended red meat and tonic wine to help restore her strength, and by the beginning of September she had improved enough for Flaubert no longer to be seriously worried. Still, he complained to the Goncourts, 'it is a nuisance and it takes up a lot of my time . . . Old people are not easy to look after.'[12] Burying himself in work on the novel helped to numb his distress. He needed treatment as much as his mother did, and writing was his chosen remedy, his 'literary vesicatory'.[13] By January 1866, Part One of *Sentimental Education* was complete.

Although he gave the work the same title as his first attempt at a novel, and although both feature two young male friends whose paths gradually diverge, Flaubert's new novel was very different from the first *Sentimental Education*. Its opening sentence, densely packed with information, seems to promise a reassuringly conventional narrative:

> On the fifteenth of September 1840, around six
> o'clock in the morning, the *Ville-de-Montereau*, on
> the point of departure, was sending up great swirling
> plumes of smoke by quai Saint-Bernard.[14]

But while seeming to root the coming narrative firmly in time and place, that confident display of facts is soon undermined. As the narrative develops, it gradually reveals a view of history grounded much less in solid data and 'real events' than in the subtle, shifting connections and confusions of everyday existence. Nevertheless, Flaubert required a mass of documentation for the project. He continued to gather information as he wrote, taking notes on aspects as diverse as fashion, fluctuations on the Paris stock exchange, racecourses, dance halls and troop movements. He talked to workmen, interviewed a policeman, quizzed his cousin about stagecoaches between Nogent-sur-Seine and Paris in 1845, enquired about the workings of small literary journals, toured porcelain factories in Creil and Sèvres, and paid a distressing visit to a hospital to observe children suffering from croup. Too late he realized that no railway line between Paris and Fontainebleau existed in 1848, and so a section of the novel had to be rewritten. At times he felt overwhelmed by the scale of the enterprise – it was, as he put it, like trying to fit the ocean into a carafe.

Moreover, money worries still nagged, for he continued to live beyond his means. Several times he tried to persuade Michel Lévy to pay him a bonus because of *Salammbô*'s continuing success, and he also appealed to his lawyer and then to Jules Duplan, begging them to find someone willing to lend him 6,000 francs, to be repaid in a few years' time. Unsuccessful there, as well as in extracting extra money from Lévy for *Salammbô*, he demanded an advance for *Sentimental Education*, but this, too, his publisher refused, offering instead to issue promissory notes. Flaubert indignantly dismissed the compromise, protesting that he would 'rather stay in Croisset *indefinitely*' on his meagre income.[15] Not until the spring of 1867 did Lévy relent and advance him 5,000 francs, by which time another of the Flaubert properties – a small farm at Courtavant – had been put up for sale. Yet another, at Pont-sur-Seine, was sold the following summer. Before long, however, Flaubert was again complaining of penury and borrowing money from Ernest Commanville, though the Goncourt brothers noticed that he was not too impoverished to have a handsome box custom-made to hold the manuscript of *Sentimental Education*.

Flaubert's financial difficulties fed into his portrayal of Frédéric's and Deslauriers' fluctuating resources and the resultant tensions in their relationship; as he told Caroline, 'I bring everything I see and feel to this work (as is my habit).'[16] But the old, disturbing images also pushed their way into the novel, surfacing, for example, in the graphic description of Monsieur Dambreuse's dead body, in Frédéric's hallucination of his own drowned corpse floating in the Seine and in his chilling vision at the fancy dress ball of 'cadavers at the morgue in their leather aprons, with the cold-water tap running over their hair'.[17]

In August 1866, on the recommendation of Sainte-Beuve and Princesse Mathilde, Flaubert was awarded the Legion of Honour – the same decoration that he had cynically bestowed on Homais at the end of *Madame Bovary* to mark the triumph of mediocrity. The irony cannot have been lost on him, but he accepted the honour graciously, pleased to be awarded it alongside Hippolyte Taine and gratified by the messages of congratulations that arrived from friends. Although working apace on his novel, Flaubert was far from socially isolated. In addition to the visitors who called at his Paris apartment on the boulevard du Temple on his regular 'at home' Sundays, there were frequent dinners with friends, visits to both his nieces and another expedition to London that summer to see Juliet Herbert. In September George Sand spent several days as his guest at Croisset, charming Madame Flaubert and sending her host a thank-you gift of all 75 volumes of her collected works. On that occasion Flaubert read *The Temptation of St Anthony* aloud to her, and when she returned for a longer visit in November, for several hours each evening he read her *The Castle of Hearts* and long sections of *Sentimental Education*, which they discussed late into the night.

Paris, meanwhile, was full of preparations for the Exposition universelle of 1867, designed as an international display of the achievements of the French Empire. Although he declined Princess Mathilde's invitation to view it with her before its public opening on 1 April, Flaubert had visited it twice by early May and went again in August with his mother. He found the exhibition overwhelming and alien, as if he had been transported into some ugly new world of the future, but as a showcase of 'industrial art' it chimed with the world of *Sentimental Education*. Industrial art was a concept abhorrent to Flaubert, a contradiction in terms, an abomination that epitomized his contemporaries' lack of artistic sensibility and individual creativity; in *Sentimental Education*, he depicts the brash Monsieur Arnoux as a dealer in such mass-produced artefacts.

On those visits to the exhibition, Flaubert could not have missed the massive displays of military equipment that filled the exhibition park, where the world's largest and most powerful cannon, the centrepiece of Prussia's exhibit, was trained directly on the exhibition palace. The Prussian cannon appeared to confirm the contemporary cliché that 'dark clouds were gathering on the horizon.' The worrying rise of Prussia as a European power, France's ill-fated military intervention in Mexico and the

Part of the Prussian display, including a Krupp cannon, at the 1867 Exposition universelle in Paris.

ensuing execution of Emperor Maximilian, as well as widespread strikes and workers' unrest at home, all contributed to a general sense of foreboding. But Flaubert was dismissive of what he considered to be bourgeois anxieties. (Princess Mathilde often asked Flaubert to explain what he meant by the word *bourgeois* and concluded it simply stood for anything he disliked.) In this case he assured friends, 'The bourgeoisie are frightened of everything. Frightened of war, frightened of workers' strikes, frightened of the (probable) death of the Prince Imperial. It's a universal panic.'[18] The prevailing national mood reminded him of his compatriots' stupidity in 1848, and reinforced his contempt for both. The more he researched the revolutionary period for his novel, and the more he learned about the Catholic Church's 'enormous and deplorable' influence on the events of 1848, the better he felt he understood France's current situation.[19] His anticlerical sentiments grew, and on Good Friday 1868, he took pleasure in attending a deliberately provocative dinner organized by Sainte-Beuve at which the richest of dishes – crayfish, salmon trout, beef fillet and truffled pheasant – were served in defiance of the Church's rules on fasting, much to the outrage of the conservative press.

Flaubert finished Part Two of his novel in the bitterly cold January of 1868, but his elation at reaching that milepost was immediately overshadowed by yet another family tragedy. Little Jenny Roquigny, his great-niece, whose father had killed himself when she was only a few months old, died suddenly a few days after her third birthday: measles caught from her mother had quickly turned to pneumonia. Although Flaubert used to complain about the disruption whenever Juliette's boisterous offspring visited Croisset, he had been very fond of the little girl 'who twittered like a bird', and he was greatly saddened by her death.[20] The anguish of Juliette and Achille distressed him too, but to his surprise, Madame Flaubert, who had watched four of her own children die, seemed to bear the loss of her great-granddaughter with quiet acceptance.

Work on *Sentimental Education* continued. There was more archival research to be done in Paris, as well as visits to places Flaubert wanted to inspect, including the forest of Fontainebleau, Père Lachaise cemetery, a maternity clinic and the home of a wet nurse. He took particular care to gather details for scenes involving Rosanette and Frédéric's baby – that short-lived child of the revolution whose death shortly before the coup d'état embodies the end of so many ideals – and he appealed to Joanny Maisiat (who had earlier advised on Pellerin's portrait of Rosanette) for ideas about the kind of insensitive reflections on art that Pellerin might utter while painting the baby's decomposing corpse.

Not until April 1869, however, did Flaubert settle on the novel's title. To George Sand, whom he had asked for suggestions, he wrote,

This is the one I have adopted as a last resort: *Sentimental Education, the Story of a Young Man*. I am not saying it is good. But so far it is the one that best conveys the thought behind the book.[21]

Flaubert worried that the difficulty of finding a title meant that the novel lacked focus, but it was too late for such misgivings. At 4:56 in the morning of 16 May he scribbled an excited note to Jules Duplan: 'FINISHED! . . . Yes, my book is finished!'[22]

Princess Mathilde was eager to be the first to hear the new novel, and after much persuasion, Flaubert agreed to read the first three chapters aloud at her salon the following week. His reading met with such acclaim from guests that the princess insisted that he continue to the end, in five four-hour sessions. Much of his success, he felt, was due to the way he had read; he reported to Caroline that his dramatic rendition had impressed even himself. There were still revisions to be made, however. Du Camp suggested several large cuts and many minor alterations, not all of which Flaubert accepted. But Bouilhet, who had been so intimately involved with the novel, and so crucial in advising on revisions for Flaubert's previous novels, was unable to help. He had been ailing and exhausted and uncharacteristically morose for some time, and Flaubert now feared that his friend might be seriously ill. Visiting him in Rouen at the end of June, Flaubert found him surrounded by doctors, who could offer no diagnosis but recommended a recuperative stay in Vichy. Soon, however, it became clear there would be no recovery, and on 19 July Flaubert received a telegram announcing that Bouilhet had died the previous evening.

The death of Bouihet came as a devastating blow. Flaubert had lost not only an intimate friend whom he had known since school days and with whom he had shared endless lewd jokes, confidences and gossip, but an invaluable adviser and critic whose acute literary sensibility he greatly admired. When Bouilhet was laid to rest near the Flaubert family's burial plot in Rouen cemetery, Flaubert felt as if he had buried part of himself. Grief-stricken notes made the following day reveal the extent to which he experienced the bereavement not only as the loss of a friend, but as a literary deprivation: 'What a loss! What an irreparable loss! What unerring taste! What ingenuity! How well he clarified my ideas! What a critic! What a master! With his death, I have lost my literary compass.'[23]

In his despair, he wondered whether there was any point in continuing to write now that Bouilhet was no longer there. He persevered with the revisions, however – a task he would once have done alongside Bouilhet – and less than a month later Michel Lévy received the manuscript of *Sentimental Education*. Excited articles anticipating the arrival of a new novel by Gustave Flaubert soon began to appear in the press. Before its publication, however, Flaubert was shaken by another death: that of Sainte-Beuve, the great critic for whom he had, in part, written *Sentimental Education*. Flaubert's small group of kindred spirits had dwindled even further. He felt as if he were one of the few remaining survivors on a literary version of the raft of the *Medusa*, adrift in a hostile world, now that his forthcoming novel had lost two of its most perceptive and sympathetic readers. '[Sainte-Beuve] will have died without knowing a line of it! Bouilhet never heard the last two chapters! So much for our plans!'[24]

When *Sentimental Education* finally went on sale in November 1869, it met with reviews that were almost universally hostile. Taking particular exception to the episode where Monsieur Roque shoots a prisoner at the Tuileries, some Rouen citizens suspected Flaubert of using the novel to stir up revolutionary fervour and demanded that such books be banned. Others compared him to the Marquis de Sade. Some recipients of a personal copy of the novel avoided all mention of it. Although Flaubert had earlier told George Sand that neither patriots nor reactionaries would forgive him for writing the book, he was shocked to discover the degree of animosity he had aroused. A month after its publication, however, despite the reviews and despite its politics, he was able to report that *Sentimental Education* was selling extremely well.

Flaubert around the time that *Sentimental Education* was published. (Photograph attributed to Nadar).

8

Struggles and Defeats, 1869–74

GERMANS. Nation of dreamers (*archaic*). It's not
surprising that they beat us, we weren't ready!
Gustave Flaubert, *Dictionary of Received Ideas*

For Flaubert, the loss of Bouilhet was like 'a major amputation'.[1]
He threw himself into the task of preserving and promoting the
legacy of a friend whose literary accomplishments had never
received the recognition he believed they deserved. Bouilhet had
left instructions that four of his friends, including Flaubert, Du
Camp and d'Osmoy, should decide what was to be done with his
unpublished work, and so two days after the funeral, Flaubert
collected all Bouilhet's papers from his long-term companion,
Léonie Leparfait, and her son Philippe, and began to sift through
them. Within the week, he found himself appointed president of
a commission formed with the aim of erecting a monument to
Bouilhet in Rouen, and he set about organizing a fundraising event
at Paris's Odéon theatre, which had already provisionally agreed to
stage Bouilhet's play *Mademoiselle Aïssé*. Flaubert was also eager to
publish a collection of Bouilhet's poems and to arrange for another
play, *Heart on the Right* (*Le coeur à droite*), to be performed. Making
decisions about Bouilhet's papers, planning a preface for an edition
of his poems, negotiating with publishers and theatre directors,
and coordinating the memorial appeal were initially welcome
distractions for Flaubert, but they soon turned into a protracted

and frustrating series of battles as he fought to consolidate his friend's literary reputation. Meanwhile, he had also to contend with the stress of moving to a new apartment, for he could no longer afford to rent the flat on the boulevard du Temple. He found a smaller, fourth-floor apartment on rue Murillo, overlooking the Parc Monceau and not too far from Caroline and Ernest's new house on rue de Clichy, but it required renovation work, which seemed to drag on forever, and when he finally vacated the old flat, with all its happy associations, it was with a heavy heart.

Although Flaubert sensed that it would do him good to plunge back into his new version of *The Temptation of St Anthony*, these disruptions made it almost impossible for him to write. The death of Jules Duplan, who had been almost as close to him as Bouilhet, came as another crushing blow in March 1870. George Sand, warm and sympathetic as ever, invited Flaubert to stay with her family in the country for a few days, but he refused – country air was not the answer to his grief. Now suffering not only from his habitual eczema and boils but from flu, he felt sick in mind and body, and frequently found himself dissolving into tears. For the first time, he sensed the approach of old age. Renewed worries about money added to his distress, for his prolonged stay in Paris had again sent him into debt, and he had borrowed several thousand francs from his old travelling companion, Dr Cloquet, making him promise never to mention the loan to Madame Flaubert.

In early May 1870 Flaubert returned to Croisset to begin the painful task of composing a homage to Bouilhet to serve as a preface for *Last Songs* (*Dernières chansons*), the selection of his friend's poems that he and Du Camp had prepared for publication. Leafing through old letters and rereading all Bouilhet's work stirred up poignant memories, and as he wrote, he constantly had to choke back sobs. Although relieved to have left his Parisian responsibilities behind, Flaubert found life in Croisset cheerless. 'When I leave my study, it is to eat alone with my mother, who is as deaf as a post and interested in absolutely nothing but her health,' he told Du Camp.[2] His sense of desolation deepened a few weeks later, when he found himself at the funeral of yet another friend: this time it was that of Jules de Goncourt, who had succumbed to syphilis at the age of 39. Within a short period, four of the seven original members of the Magny dinner club – Gavarni, Bouilhet, Sainte-Beuve and Goncourt – had died, leaving Flaubert bereft. Turgenev and Sand were now the only remaining friends with whom he could seriously discuss literature and share his passions and fears.

More conscious than ever of his own mortality, and feeling that he had had 'more than [his] fill of coffins, like an old cemetery', Flaubert resolved to pay more attention to his health.[3] He began taking an energetic swim in the river every evening before dinner, and sipping glasses of tar-water. Cold baths and post prandial strolls round the vegetable garden were also part of a regimen he hoped would restore him to a state in which he could again start working seriously on *The Temptation of St Anthony*. Since Bouilhet's death, he felt he had lost his compulsion to write because he had lost the person for whom he was writing, but he was determined to begin again, and on 14 July he proudly announced that he hoped to have completed four pages by the end of the week.

Although the letters Flaubert wrote at this time rarely mention events in the wider world, he cannot have failed to notice that the 'dark storm clouds' of which he had once been so dismissive were coming ever closer. But he did not realize how close they now were. The North German Confederation, headed by Prussia, not only aimed to expand south to form a united Germany, but had staked a Prussian claim to the Spanish throne. Fearing encirclement by its powerful neighbour, and further provoked by Bismarck's notorious Ems telegram, France declared war on Prussia on 18 July 1870. As the Germans swiftly mobilized their well-trained army and invaded northeastern France,

The Temptation of St Anthony ceased to be Flaubert's priority. Instead, he directed his grief and anger at the impending carnage, sickened by what he saw as the idiocy of his fellow Frenchmen. 'The fearful butchery that is coming does not even have a pretext. It is the desire to fight for the sake of fighting,' he told George Sand.[4] Those who talked of taking revenge for Bismarck's insolence and those who cowered in terror infuriated him in equal measure: 'What stupidity! What cowardice! What ignorance! What presumption! My compatriots make me want to vomit,' he ranted. He foresaw apocalyptic consequences for the years ahead:

> Race wars are perhaps about to start again? Within a century, shall we see millions of men killing one another at one fell swoop? All the Orient against all Europe, the old world versus the new![5]

Fleeing from advancing Prussian troops, family relatives took refuge in the house at Croisset, which now had sixteen people under its roof. News from the front was sparse. Flaubert went daily to the railway station in Rouen in the hope of finding out what was happening, and, not knowing what else to do, he volunteered to help as a nurse at the Hôtel-Dieu. Despite the uncertainty and confusion, it was clear to him that France had reached a watershed and would never be the same again: 'A new world is about to begin,' he repeatedly told friends.[6] Within weeks of war being declared, the ragged French army had been decisively crushed at the Battle of Sedan, Napoléon III had surrendered and been taken prisoner, and on 4 September 1870 Léon Gambetta formally announced the fall of the Second Empire and the establishment of a French Republic. The collapse occurred so suddenly that Flaubert found it hard to believe, and he remained confident that the people of France would never capitulate, even if the Emperor had done so. Although he thought it unlikely that the Prussians would besiege

Paris, he was sure that if their troops did march on the capital, the whole nation would rise up to drive the invaders back across the Rhine. He joined Rouen's National Guard in readiness, bought himself a soldier's kitbag and took part in night patrols. Caroline, meanwhile, fled to safety in London, staying with two of her former English governesses – first Juliet Herbert and then Mrs Farmer. Her escape brought Flaubert little comfort, however. She might be safe from the Prussians in London, but he feared that exposure to the English climate and to English cuisine would destroy her health.

Sporadic news of the fighting reached Rouen by hot-air balloon and carrier pigeon, and it soon became clear that there would be no quick armistice. Seeing events from a literary perspective, Flaubert wished that he could have ended *Sentimental Education* with the captured Emperor slumped in a coach and surrounded by thousands of angry prisoners hurling insults at him. In his view, France's whole sorry mess was a consequence of what he called 'the long falsehood' of the Second Empire, when, as he reminded Du Camp, 'everything was false: false army, false politics, false literature, false credit and even false tarts – Telling the truth was immoral!'[7] Nevertheless, he remained convinced that the angry, humiliated French would triumph in the end: the nation was united, and he was certain that the situation could never disintegrate into civil war, despite English newspapers' predictions to the contrary. But within days of his confident pronouncement, with a besieged Paris running out of supplies, the Prussians closing in on Rouen and hordes of the displaced poor coming to his door in Croisset begging for food, his assurance faded. He could tell that the town's inhabitants would not resist the invaders, and the local militia under his charge proved so undisciplined that he resigned from the National Guard after only a few weeks' service. His prognostications were now bleak: 'Within a month, it will all be finished,' he told Caroline in early October. 'That is to say, the first act of the drama will be over. The second act will be civil war.'[8]

Rouen fell to the enemy on 5 December 1870. Prussian soldiers and their horses were billeted at Croisset. By then, Flaubert and his mother had abandoned the big house, but they refused to move further than Rouen, for he could not bear to be far from his books and papers, and his mother wanted to be near Achille. To Flaubert, it seemed like the end of the world. He felt as though Prussian boots were trampling over his brain, reducing him to an emotional and intellectual wreck. After having been in abeyance for several years, his epileptic symptoms returned. His mother worried about him, he worried about her, and both worried desperately about poor Caroline and urged her to return, particularly after Achille's wife told them that London had a smallpox epidemic.

When Paris finally surrendered to the Prussians at the end of January 1871, Flaubert could not contain his anger and contempt:

> It's enough to make one hang oneself in rage! I am furious that Paris did not burn down to the very last house, leaving only a big black void. France has sunk so low, is so dishonoured, so demeaned, that I wish it would disappear completely. I hope that civil war is going to kill lots of people. May I be one of them![9]

He refused to wear his Legion of Honour, telling Caroline that 'honour' was no longer a French word and that he intended to ask Turgenev about becoming Russian. His mood lightened, however, when Caroline returned from England and he took his mother to stay with her in Dieppe. The sight of his beloved niece safely back on home soil calmed them both, and the signing of the Treaty of Versailles on 26 February, though humiliating to the French, at least marked the end of hostilities.

By mid-March the situation was safe enough for Flaubert to travel to Brussels with Alexandre Dumas to visit Princess Mathilde, who had fled there when the Second Empire collapsed. While in Brussels, however, he heard news of a serious outbreak of fighting in Paris. Not only was Flaubert desperately worried in case Caroline and her husband had been caught up in the violence, but it was now impossible for him to return home via the French capital. Instead, he was forced to travel via London, where he met Juliet Herbert briefly before making a stormy ferry crossing back to Dieppe to be reunited with his mother and his niece. Although news from Paris continued to worsen as hostility between radical socialist Communards and the new national government slid into civil war, Flaubert was at last able to return to the house at Croisset. To his surprise, he found that the rooms had been left clean and orderly. The garden was full of primroses, the trees were coming into leaf, and for the first time in months, he felt at peace. That evening he resumed work on *The Temptation of St Anthony*.

It was perhaps this new-found sense of tranquillity that led him to predict that the Paris uprising would subside within days; but again he was proved wrong as the violence continued. Not until the end of May were the Communards finally crushed, in a horrific week of bloodshed – the so-called *semaine sanglante* – that left the city with over twenty thousand dead and with many of its public buildings burned to the ground. Within days of the carnage, Flaubert was back in Paris, ostensibly to continue researching *The Temptation of St Anthony*, but also to view the city's ruins, which had quickly become a tourist attraction. If Du Camp is to be believed, as he and Flaubert stood gazing at the blackened shell of the Tuileries Palace, Flaubert commented that the insurrection would never have happened if only people had fully understood *Sentimental Education*. To Caroline he described the ruined buildings as 'beautiful', 'sinister' and 'wonderful', but to George Sand he confided a more extreme reaction that was not confined to the city's structural damage:

> The stench of corpses disgusts me less than the miasma
> of egoism that emanates from every mouth. The sight of
> the ruins is as nothing compared to the immense stupidity

Ruined buildings on the rue de Rivoli, Paris, in the aftermath of the *semaine sanglante* of May 1871.

of Paris. With very few exceptions, *everyone* seemed mad enough to need a straightjacket. Half the population wants to strangle the other half, who have the same intention. You see it clearly in the eyes of passers-by.[10]

Worse still, most Parisians appeared already to have forgotten about the war, while some even spoke of the Prussians with admiration, failing to recognize that the recent killings, looting and arson in their city replicated the violence of the invasion. So outraged was Flaubert by what he had witnessed ('I would like to drown humanity in my vomit,' he told Ernest Feydeau) that for long after his visit, he found it impossible to concentrate on *The Temptation of St Anthony*.[11]

He did, however, continue in his efforts to honour Bouilhet's memory, submitting a proposal to the mayor of Rouen for a memorial fountain, putting final pre-publication touches to

Tourists viewing the burned shell of the Hotel de Ville, Paris, destroyed during the Commune.

Bouilhet's posthumous volume of poems, pressing the Odéon theatre to fulfil its commitment to stage *Mademoiselle Aïssé* and negotiating with the Comédie-Française to take on the play if the Odéon continued to prevaricate. Rehearsals for *Mademoiselle Aïssé* finally began at the Odéon in early December. Flaubert busily involved himself in every aspect, including casting, costume design, scenery and publicity, and after reading the play aloud to the cast, he attended every rehearsal, confident that the play would be a great success. Its opening night on 6 January 1872, with Sarah Bernhardt in the title role and many old friends in the audience, was a triumph. The second performance, however, played to an almost empty house. An early review dismissed the play as 'crude melodrama', and hopes that it would earn money for Bouilhet's dependents were dashed.[12] Nor was this the only disappointment, for to Flaubert's fury, Rouen's municipal council refused permission for a Bouilhet memorial fountain.

The rejection was like a red rag to a bull. Flaubert immediately set about preparing a vitriolic open letter to the council, unearthing pieces of leaden verse composed by one of its officers, collecting examples of 'imbeciles or nonentities' who had been granted monuments and lobbying journalists to express incredulity that Rouen should have vetoed a memorial to a poet of Bouilhet's calibre.[13] He would take voluptuous pleasure in making the municipal council die of shame, Flaubert told Philippe Leparfait. In a twenty-page diatribe in which anger about the insult to Bouilhet's memory merged with rage over how readily the city had capitulated to the Prussians, he poured scorn on council members who did not 'know how to hold a pen or a gun', accusing them of philistinism, cowardice and idiocy.[14] His friend Charles Lapierre, the sympathetic editor of the *Nouvelliste de Rouen*, decided that the piece was too inflammatory for his newspaper and advised publication in Paris, where the open letter duly appeared in *Le Temps* before being reissued for wider distribution as a single, slim volume. But the council refused to budge, and although today's Rouen has a memorial to Bouilhet, Flaubert did not live to see it.

These early, unstable years of the Third Republic were difficult times for Flaubert and for France. 'We are tossed between the Society of St Vincent de Paul and the Internationale,' he complained, as the Catholic Right – which saw the nation's defeat as a punishment from God – strengthened its position against the Republican Left, which in turn feared the so-called Moral Order of the Right and dreaded a return of the monarchy.[15] But for Flaubert, personal worries loomed even larger. Once again, the most pressing involved money, but this time the problem was far more serious than before. Ernest Commanville had speculated on the price of timber in the expectation that it would rise, but the market had crashed and he was forced to sell at a heavy loss. His business was failing, and the shameful prospect of bankruptcy hung over not only Caroline and Ernest but Flaubert himself, since much of his capital was tied up in the Commanville business. Princess Mathilde, to whom he confided his difficulty, offered to raise the necessary sum by mortgaging her residence at St Gratien, but this was far too generous an offer for Flaubert to accept, and he continued to search desperately for some other means of solving the problem. 'The life I have led this winter would have killed three rhinoceroses,' he moaned in February 1872.[16] So when he discovered the following month that Michel Lévy had failed to honour what he considered to have been a firm agreement to pay the printing costs of Bouilhet's *Last Songs*, Flaubert was in no mood to negotiate. Feeling bitter and betrayed, he confronted Lévy, and in a furious outburst accused him of dishonesty and terminated their professional relationship forthwith. By Flaubert's own admission, his outrage 'bordered on madness', and he felt ill for days afterwards.[17] So angry did he remain that when Lévy was awarded the Legion of Honour a year later, Flaubert once more unpinned his own decoration in protest, and refused to wear it again until after Lévy's death.

The incident added to his sense of failure and humiliation. 'When one has given all one's heart, mind, nerves, muscles and time for nothing, one falls back, completely crushed,' he confided to George Sand, adding that it was perhaps just as well that poor Bouilhet had died, and that he was determined to have no further dealings with printers, editors or newspapers for many years to come:

> I have failed in everything this winter. *Aïssé* made no money. *Last Songs* nearly ended in a lawsuit against Lévy. The business with the fountain is still not over . . . Let's hope I don't also fail with *St Anthony*![18]

Although he continued to collect material for *The Temptation of St Anthony*, Flaubert felt too defeated to resume writing. Sand's suggestion that he might find solace in marriage was dismissed out of hand. Moreover, his mother, now 78, frail and very deaf, was another source of distress, for the Prussian invasion and the occupation of her home had taken their toll. Increasingly depressed and irritable, and demanding constant company, she worried and exasperated her son in equal measure. He and Caroline decided to employ a lady's companion for her, but finding someone suitable proved difficult. Madame Flaubert had been staying with the Commanvilles in Dieppe while Flaubert was in Paris and while decorators worked on the Croisset house, but towards the end of March she insisted on returning home, even though the house was still in disarray and smelled strongly of wet paint. Still reeling from his quarrel with Lévy, Flaubert left Paris to receive her, and was alarmed at how rapidly she seemed to be deteriorating. He anticipated a bleak summer spent in her company, but on 6 April 1872, just over a week after her return to Croisset, Madame Flaubert died.

Flaubert now realized just how much he had loved his mother. Her death left him feeling eviscerated, and he was barely able to

Bust of Gustave Flaubert's mother, from the original by E. Guilbert, 1873.

respond to the messages of sympathy that arrived from friends. Compounding his grief was a new uncertainty about his future, for in her will his mother had left the Croisset house to Caroline, with the proviso that Flaubert should have continuing use of his study and bedroom as long as he remained unmarried. But Caroline already had homes in Dieppe and Paris and would not want to live in the Croisset house, which was too big and very costly to run; might she decide to sell it? If so, what would he do? Where would he go? These doubts tormented him, though he recognized that he experienced suffering more acutely than most people did. He was, in his telling phrase, 'by nature a flayed man'.[19]

Knowing that the only solution for his troubled mind was to lose himself in work, at the end of April he forced himself to resume work on *The Temptation of St Anthony*. It was more of a struggle than ever. His heart was not in it, and he was still caught up in complex financial matters, much against his will. Nevertheless, he was determined to complete the book that had preoccupied him ever since Breughel's painting had held him spellbound in Genoa in 1845.

Part of this extraordinary project's appeal for Flaubert was that it allowed him to explore the full breadth and power of his imagination while letting him pursue the idea of relative truth. His years of reading about Oriental heresies, philosophy and religion are transformed into St Anthony's hallucinations. The text refuses to evaluate or explain the philosophical positions with which the saint grapples, and everything is presented as a construct of Anthony's mind. As the Devil points out to him, 'things come to you only through the intermediary of your mind. Like a concave mirror, it distorts objects – and you have no means of verifying them.'[20] In this strange and all-consuming work, the saint resists all attempts to force him out of isolation in the desert. He wrestles with the full array of human passions – embodied and magnified by the seven deadly sins – and is assailed by monstrous creatures from land, sea and air until the known world gradually dissolves into one great cosmic life force. Anthony's final cry resonates with Flaubert's own agonizingly impossible aspiration as a writer: 'I would like . . . to vibrate like sound, shine like light, crouch within every form, penetrate each atom, descend to the very depths of matter – be matter itself!'[21] On 1 July 1872, nearly quarter of a century after his first attempts at the project, Flaubert finally announced, 'I have finished *St Anthony*! Thank God!'[22] Unwilling to consider publication after the dispute with Lévy, however, he consigned the manuscript to a drawer.

Within a week, he and Caroline had travelled to Bagnères-de-Luchon, a fashionable spa resort near the Spanish border where the pair hoped that taking the waters and spending a restful month in the fresh mountain air of the Pyrenees would do them both good. Nevertheless, Flaubert arrived with plans for work. Among Bouilhet's papers he had found the draft of a play, *The Weaker Sex* (*Le Sexe faible*), which two Paris theatres had already turned down but which he intended to revise and develop, and he also wanted to think more about the long-term project that would eventually become *Bouvard and Pécuchet*. He did not settle easily into his new environment, complaining of noise, boredom and being surrounded by annoying bourgeois. The spa doctor blamed his nervous irritability on too much tobacco, a diagnosis Flaubert found absurd, though he was too polite to say so. Writing in such surroundings was almost impossible, and apart from bathing and sipping spa water, there was little for him to do: he paid several visits to a nearby zoo, read Charles Dickens's *The Pickwick Papers* (whose fine qualities he thought ruined by the 'defective composition' characteristic of English novels) and enjoyed an excursion into the wild countryside bordering on Spain, 'far removed from the *bourgeois*, from falseness and from all the rotten filth of modern life'.[23] It sparked glimmers of his old wanderlust, and for a brief moment he entertained the improbable fantasy of continuing south on foot all the way to Madrid.

Soon, however, he was back in his Croisset study, making extensive revisions to Bouilhet's ironically titled *The Weaker Sex*. Bouilhet had told Flaubert about his idea for this play in 1864 and had outlined its misogynistic viewpoint: it was to 'show all the cowardly acts that women make us commit, and the terrible power they wrongfully assume, day by day, in the most important matters in the world'. That, Bouilhet had believed, was 'the sign of the times'.[24] Over the coming months Flaubert immersed himself in the project, hoping that this time the play would raise some money for the Leparfaits and pleased to be once again engaged in matters theatrical. Indeed, he so enjoyed the process of adapting ideas for the stage and turning thoughts into dialogue that in July 1873 he embarked on a play of his own, *The Candidate* (*Le Candidat*), a bleakly satirical attack on bourgeois materialism, immorality and self-interest that focuses on the central character's burning ambition to become a deputy, regardless of political affiliation. Producing such a cynical piece – arguably the most misanthropic text he ever wrote – clearly suited Flaubert's dark mood at this time. He found it '*enormously* enjoyable', and for once, the writing came easily.[25]

Paris's Théâtre du Vaudeville expressed interest in *The Weaker Sex*. The manager, Léon Carvalho, assured Flaubert that it would be a huge success and talked of scheduling it for the winter of 1873. When Carvalho heard about *The Candidate*, however, the prospect of staging a work by the famous Gustave Flaubert proved more enticing than a play by Louis Bouilhet, and he found reasons to postpone *The Weaker Sex*. *The Candidate*, on the other hand, was revised, publicized and rehearsed, and after narrowly passing the censors' scrutiny, it finally had its premiere on 11 March 1874. Although Flaubert bought seats for many of his friends to ensure a good opening night, not even their supportive presence could disguise the fact that the play was a disaster. The audience booed and whistled; in his journal, Edmond de Goncourt expressed dismay at the work's lack of taste, tact and originality; and the reviews were savage. After seeing the male lead come off stage in tears on the second night, Flaubert withdrew *The Candidate* after only four performances. He put on a brave face, blaming the public for being too stupid to understand him, but it was another humiliating and expensive defeat.

The Weaker Sex fared no better. The Vaudeville decided not to stage it after all, the Odéon turned it down, and although the director of the Théâtre de Cluny sounded enthusiastic and predicted a great financial success, Flaubert withdrew the play at the last moment when he realized how badly it would be performed. Further attempts to have it staged proved fruitless, leaving him permanently disenchanted with Parisian theatre. Apart from the occasional further attempt to interest a director in *The Castle of Hearts*, Flaubert's long love affair with the stage had come to a bitter end.

After the rupture with Michel Lévy, Flaubert had entered into an agreement with the young publisher Georges Charpentier, who had recently taken over his father's publishing house, and in December 1873, despite previous misgivings, he entrusted the manuscript of *The Temptation of St Anthony* to him. Two weeks after the humiliating closure of *The Candidate*, the book that Flaubert described as his 'whole life's work' finally appeared in print, dedicated to the memory of Alfred Le Poittevin, and within days it had sold two thousand copies, to the great delight of author and publisher.[26] Soon, however, the reviews appeared. Although critics in England and Germany had good things to say, the French press was hostile. Particularly vicious was Saint-René Taillandier in the *Revue des deux mondes*, who sneered, 'The last book he published was deadly boring; this one is unreadable.'[27] '*It's going well*. The insults are piling up!' Flaubert reported to George Sand.[28] Although he tried to shrug off the attacks, it was clear that his disdain for bourgeois mediocrity and for the artistic taste of his contemporaries had won him few friends in the

French literary establishment. He realized that although reviewers criticized the work, the attacks were aimed at him personally:

> My God! Aren't they stupid! What asses! And underneath, I can feel *hatred* directed at myself. Why? Whom have I hurt? It can all be explained in a word: *I am bothersome*; and I am bothersome less with my pen than with my character.[29]

The critics' hostility merely reinforced his conviction that his contemporaries no longer understood or valued literature, although the few people whose opinions he respected, including Victor Hugo and Ernest Renan, recognized *The Temptation of St Anthony* as a work of exceptional quality. '[Critics] can say what they like. *St Anthony* is a masterpiece, a magnificent book,' Sand assured him. 'Rejoice in the insults, they promise great things for the future.'[30] But, particularly since the recent deaths of Théophile Gautier and Ernest Feydeau, Flaubert felt as if he belonged to an increasingly endangered species that struggled to survive in a hostile environment. He and a small group of like-minded writers who had suffered similar attacks – Turgenev, Zola, Edmond de Goncourt and Alphonse Daudet – took to meeting regularly for mutual support at what they defiantly referred to as 'dinners for booed authors'.

Flaubert's recent disappointments had left him feeling utterly drained, however. Calling him 'a hysterical old woman', his doctor prescribed another spa visit, and so at the end of June 1874 Flaubert dutifully travelled to Rigi Kaltbad, in the Swiss Alps, for a three-week cure.[31] He was not the ideal patient. 'The beauties of Nature bore me deeply,' he wrote to Caroline, 'My consolation is to stuff myself with food and to smoke. Oh! I certainly smoke all right!'[32] But although he detested the enforced tedium, he had to admit that mountain air, sound sleep and gentle exercise were having a beneficial effect. His headaches vanished, his complexion lost its unhealthy flush, and he began to think about literary plans for the future.

9

The Final Years, 1874–80

BUDGET. Never balanced.

Gustave Flaubert, *Dictionary of Received Ideas*

On his return to Croisset, Flaubert arranged his pens neatly on his desk and, after 'a whole afternoon of torture', produced the opening sentence of *Bouvard and Pécuchet*.[1] He had been mulling over ideas for this novel for many years, and had told Madame Roger des Genettes in 1872 that it was to be

> the story of these two fellows who copy – it's a kind of critical encyclopaedia in the form of a joke . . . For it, I shall have to study many things I know nothing about: chemistry, medicine, agriculture . . . You have to be stark raving mad to undertake a book like this![2]

Flaubert was aware of having embarked on an enormous and perhaps impossible enterprise, but as he told Caroline, the important thing was that it would occupy his mind for years to come, for 'while you are working, you do not think about your own wretched self.'[3] To begin with, all went well. Earlier in the summer of 1874, Flaubert had toured Lower Normandy with his friend Edmond Laporte, the manager of a Rouen lace factory, in search of a suitable location for Bouvard and

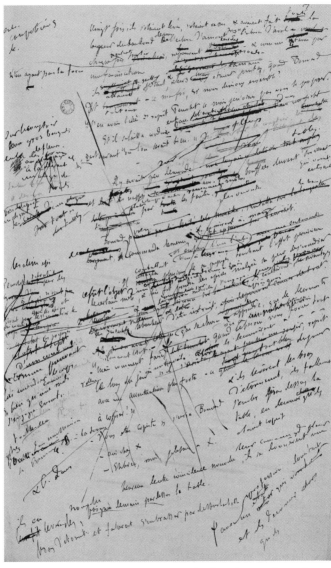

Manuscript draft from the first chapter of *Bouvard and Pécuchet*; Brouillons, vol. 1, folio 21v.

Pécuchet's house. He had selected a spot 'on a stupid plateau between Caen and Falaise', and by mid-October the first chapter was complete, with his two clerks happily ensconced in Chavignolles.[4] Chapter Two was to have them launch themselves into a series of projects involving agriculture, arboriculture, horticulture, canning, preserving and distilling, all of which required extensive research on Flaubert's part. He visited a model farm, consulted experts, and read and read.

Soon, however, the magnitude of his task began to overwhelm him. He wondered again if he had been insane to tackle such a project. Moreover, he constantly felt ill and irritable, without being able to put his finger on what was wrong. Perhaps, he mused to George Sand, he was suffering from the ills of France itself. In an attempt to settle his nerves, he gave up coffee and forced himself to take daily exercise, but he was trapped in a vicious circle, working as hard as possible on the novel in order to take his mind off his inner turmoil, yet aware that the scale and difficulty of the project only added to his distress. His symptoms were both physical and mental: coughs, colds, headaches, strange pains and frequent tears. Two doctors examined him and prescribed potassium bromide, commonly used at the time as a sedative to treat epileptic seizures and nervous disorders. Although it calmed him, the side effects caused disfiguring patches of eczema to appear on his face. At 53, Flaubert felt old and worn out, and overwhelmed by unbidden memories from long ago. 'The *Past* is devouring me,' he told Madame Roger des Genettes, 'and I no longer expect anything of the Future, anything at all.'[5] Memories of his Oriental journey crowded in, contributing to his sense of travelling across an endless desert towards an unknown destination. He saw himself not only as the traveller but as the empty wasteland and the slow, burdened camel.

Solitude became increasingly hard to bear, and so in May 1875 he exchanged the Paris flat on rue Murillo for a fifth-floor apartment next to Caroline and Ernest on rue du Faubourg Saint-Honoré. The Commanvilles' worsening financial situation added to his distress, and, fearing that his niece and her husband were concealing the full extent of their disaster, he begged them to be frank. In late July, he confided the desperate situation to Ivan Turgenev:

> I must tell you the truth: my Commanville nephew is *absolutely* ruined! And I am going to find myself very badly affected. What makes me despair in all this is the position of my poor niece! My (paternal) heart is suffering cruelly. Very sad days are beginning: lack of money, humiliation, our lives turned upside down. It is total. – And my brain is wrecked.[6]

Writing had become impossible. *Bouvard and Pécuchet* was abandoned as Flaubert channelled all his energies into limiting the financial damage as best he could, while close friends rallied round to help. Deeply concerned about his mental state, George Sand made tentative enquiries about finding him some lucrative position that would provide an income and at the same time force him to take on the duties and responsibilities of regular employment – something he had never experienced, and which she believed would do him good. Others tried to secure him a pension from the state, but Flaubert was too proud to accept, for he knew the details would be made public, and he could already imagine the reaction of the press. His own drastic solution was to sell his last remaining piece of property – the farm at Deauville inherited from his mother – and to use the proceeds to pay off Commanville's most pressing debt, arranging for Caroline's husband to give him cash when needed. '*Honour is saved!*' he assured Princess Mathilde.[7] Although substantial debts remained and the future of the Croisset house was still in doubt, bankruptcy had been averted, at least for the time being.

With the farm transaction finalized, Flaubert decided that a change of scene might help to calm his nerves. In mid-September he travelled to the fishing port of Concarneau in Brittany, where his friend Georges Pouchet, the son of the director of Rouen's Muséum d'histoire naturelle, ran a centre for marine research. For the first few days of his trip Flaubert's hands shook so much that even writing a letter was difficult, and to his embarrassment he could not control his tears. Gazing at the fish in Pouchet's aquarium, bathing in the sea, eating well and taking long walks by the shore were not enough to prevent him from worrying about the future, yet the healthier lifestyle soothed the worst of his anguish and gradually his thoughts returned to writing – not to the huge *Bouvard and Pécuchet* project, which he recognized was beyond him in his current state, but to the short story about St Julian that he had begun in 1856. George Sand, who had never liked the sound of *Bouvard and Pécuchet*, was relieved to hear that he had abandoned the ambitious novel. 'Write something more down-to-earth that will suit everyone,' she urged, and she assured him that if ever the Croisset house had to be put up for sale, she would buy it for him to live in.[8]

There followed a period of relative calm for Flaubert. After spending six weeks in Concarneau, he returned to Paris and settled into a more balanced existence, combining writing with seeing old friends and going to the theatre. Maupassant, Zola, Edmond de Goncourt, Daudet and Turgenev were regular Sunday visitors to the rue du Faubourg Saint-Honoré, and by the year's end a restructuring of Commanville's remaining debts had allayed Flaubert's worst fears.

He finished *The Legend of St Julian the Hospitaller* (*La Légende de saint Julien l'Hospitalier*) in February 1876. Although the tale was inspired in part by a stained-glass window in Rouen Cathedral representing the life of the saint, and although he had described it to Sand as the kind of 'silly little piece' that mothers would be happy to let their daughters read, Flaubert's version of St Julian's life was no ordinary hagiography.[9] In this terrible yet hauntingly beautiful tale, set in a timeless, mythic past, he blended the traditional story with elements from fairy tales and with shocking scenes of carnage as Julian massacres hundreds of wild creatures in a series of frenzied killings that culminate in the accidental murder of his parents. Yet there is something of Flaubert and his own literary struggle and sense of self-sacrifice in the tormented saint who battles to row his little boat across stormy waters that are 'blacker than ink', overwhelmed by images of death and memories of the past and driven by forces he does not understand.[10] Nor is it fortuitous that the tale's redemptive ending should have the saint embrace a leper, a figure to which Flaubert frequently likens himself in his letters.

No sooner was *The Legend of St Julian the Hospitaller* completed than Flaubert embarked on a second short story, *A Simple Heart*, with the intention of publishing both together in a single volume that autumn. The new tale was written with George Sand firmly in mind, for she had recently tried to persuade her friend to reconsider his impersonal, satirical mode of writing, which she believed alienated his readers. Flaubert painted a world that was unrelievedly dark and depressing, and he concentrated too much on stylistic perfection, she claimed. Feeling misunderstood, Flaubert defended his artistic principles: merely having fine feelings was not enough for an artist, who should always remain invisible to the reader; style and substance were inseparable. In his writing, he sought beauty above all else, he insisted:

> This concern for external Beauty for which you reproach me is, for me, a *method*. When I discover an ugly assonance or a repetition in one of my sentences, I know that I am floundering in Falsity; by searching, I find the right expression which was the only true one – and is at the same time harmonious – One never lacks a word if one has fully grasped the idea.[11]

I try to think well *in order to* write well. But it is writing well that is my aim, and I don't try to hide that.[12]

Although their exchange was something of a dialogue of the deaf, Flaubert assured Sand that she would recognize her influence in his new tale and would appreciate its humanity. In June 1876, however, with the story only half-written, George Sand died, leaving yet another wretched void in Flaubert's intellectual and emotional life. Sobbing in the rain at her funeral in a small country cemetery, ankle-deep in mud, he felt as if he were burying his mother a second time. 'My heart is turning into a necropolis,' he told Princess Mathilde. 'The void gapes ever wider!'[13]

Once again, writing was his consolation. Returning to Croisset, he settled into a routine, seeing no one, avoiding newspapers, smoking until his mouth hurt and bellowing his completed sentences into the silence of his study. Every evening, he swam in the river before dinner and then continued writing late into the night. Even as he slept, long sentences rumbled through his mind 'like the chariots of a Roman emperor', sometimes jolting him awake with their awkward cadences.[14] By mid-August, *A Simple Heart* was finished. As he described it to Madame Roger des Genettes, it was

> quite simply the story of an obscure life, that of a poor country girl, pious but not mystical, quietly devoted, and as tender-hearted as fresh bread. In succession, she loves a man, her mistress's children, a nephew, an old man she looks after, then her parrot – and when the parrot dies, she has it stuffed – and when she in turn is dying, she confuses the parrot with the Holy Spirit. It is not at all ironic, as you imagine, but on the contrary, very serious and very sad. I want to arouse pity and make sensitive souls weep, being one myself.[15]

But that account fails to convey the subtle complexity of the tale, with its perfectly poised ambiguity that allows the reader to see

Stuffed Amazonian parrot from the Musée Flaubert in Rouen.

the servant Félicité as either simple-minded or saintly, and with its multiple layers of meaning, whereby the parrot becomes, among other things, an emblem of both the limitations and the potentially transfigurative glory of language. An accurate physical description of the bird was nevertheless vital to Flaubert. In July he visited the Rouen Muséum d'histoire naturelle to inspect its parrot collection, and returned home having borrowed three books about parrots, as well as a stuffed Amazonian specimen, which he stood on his desk 'in order to fill [his] soul with parrot' while he wrote.[16]

Almost immediately after completing *A Simple Heart*, Flaubert began to prepare a third tale to accompany the two others, this time featuring the imprisonment and death of John the Baptist. The idea for *Hérodias* had come to him while writing *A Simple Heart*, and he intended its scope to be broad and politically resonant. If the tale had its roots in biblical times, its ramifications reached down through the ages, as he explained to Madame Roger des Genettes:

> The story of *Hérodias*, as I understand it, has nothing to do with religion. What I find seductive about it is the official face of Herod (who was a real *préfet*) and the wild figure of Hérodias, a kind of [Madame de] Maintenon and Cleopatra. The Racial question dominated everything.[17]

As usual, he carried out intensive research before starting to write, and as usual, writing was a struggle. Flaubert worried particularly over his description of Salomé's seductive dance, with its echoes of Kuchuk-Hanem's erotic undulations, and culminating in the strange, acrobatic pose of the little figure of Salomé carved on Rouen Cathedral's west facade. 'I need to look at a freshly severed human head,' he announced to Caroline, not entirely facetiously, in a letter in which he also discussed arrangements for a reindeer head to be mounted on the wall of his room.[18]

Sculpture of Salomé dancing on her hands, from the facade of Rouen Cathedral.

If Flaubert's incisive irony was moderated in the *Three Tales* (*Trois contes*), the title under which *St Julian*, *A Simple Heart* and *Hérodias* were published in 1877, it found a ready outlet in a major but more tentative project for which he had been making notes ever since his stay at Rigi Kaltbad in 1874, when he had had the idea of writing 'a big book in three parts, which will be called *Sous Napoléon III*'.[19] Scattered notes and plans are all that exist of *Sous Napoléon III*, but Flaubert kept returning to the venture throughout his remaining years, rearranging and revising elements of the plot while he worked on other projects. Writer friends, including Émile Zola (who had already embarked on his great series of *Rougon-Macquart* novels, set under the Second Empire), encouraged him to write about that period, knowing of his associations with the imperial court and with other major figures of the regime, and aware, too, that he had kept notes of his visits to the Tuileries Palace and Compiègne.

On one level, Flaubert's embryonic novel seems, as its title suggests, to be about France during the Second Empire, whose duration it spans: it opens with the main character refusing to swear an oath of allegiance to the new regime and ends with him dying in the Commune. Its impetus, however, came mainly from more recent and more personal sources. The fragmentary, shifting plans, featuring characters based on friends and acquaintances ranging from Henrietta Collier to a doctor he encountered at the Luchon spa in 1872, provided a space into which Flaubert could pour his personal resentment, unhappiness and rage. Memories of Bouilhet haunt the plans: the novel is partly set in his home town of Mantes, and the main character is a poet turned playwright whose literary talents go unrecognized, whose plays are not performed and who in one version dies exhausted by the constant, fruitless struggle. The theatrical world, one of the novel's central strands, is presented as a place of exploitation and disappointment that purveys false values and is run only for financial gain, and the theme announced at the outset – 'The degradation of man by woman' – echoes the misogyny of *The Weaker Sex*.[20] The work's other main strands were to focus on right-wing Catholic politics and on the world of business and financial ruin, both targets for Flaubert's irony and vilification. Moreover, in a surprising deviation from his normal practice, he planned to give each chapter a moralizing title designed to tell readers what to think, thereby implying that he was writing for a public incapable of independent judgement.

The personal, volatile nature of these little-known notes and plans suggest that they provided Flaubert with a means of venting some of the bitterness and frustration that overwhelmed him throughout the 1870s. Pressing personal concerns that had no place either in *Bouvard and Pécuchet* or in the tightly controlled *Three Tales* could be shaped and contained within its plot. Had it gone beyond the planning stage, *Sous Napoléon III* would have been Flaubert's bleakest, sourest work.

Within days of finishing *Hérodias* in early February 1877, Flaubert left Croisset for Paris, where he busied himself with arranging the publication of the *Three Tales*, canvassing support for a memorial to George Sand, making more unsuccessful attempts to place *The Castle of Hearts*, and seeing friends – including the actress Sarah Bernhardt, who tried to flatter him into letting her sculpt his features. So much hectic activity exhausted him. 'Too many errands, too many carriages, too many dinners!' he sighed.[21] He was nevertheless satisfied and rather proud to have negotiated respectable sums for his *Three Tales*, and after individual serialization in *Le Moniteur* and *Le Bien public*, the stories went on sale at the end of April in a single volume, its printing and layout meticulously supervised by Flaubert.

The publication's timing was not ideal. On this occasion, competition came not from another volume by Victor Hugo but from a French constitutional crisis. Only days after the *Three Tales* arrived in bookshops, President MacMahon, a conservative Catholic monarchist, dismissed his prime minister and used his presidential prerogative to dissolve parliament, forcing a new election in the hope of gaining a royalist majority. Although Flaubert was greatly relieved when the result showed a clear rejection of the Moral Order and its royalist ambitions, at the height of the *seize mai* crisis he was more concerned with its effect on book sales. 'My poor book has been completely flattened,' he moaned, 'The 1870 war killed off *Sentimental Education*, and now an internal *coup d'état* is paralysing the *Three Tales*.'[22] But the tales were well received, even by the normally unsympathetic *Figaro*; Russian and German translations were soon under way, and to Flaubert's amused delight, a Catholic bookshop featured the volume in its list of recommended family reading.

Flaubert returned to Croisset at the end of May, pleased to be back in his peaceful old study with its leafy view over the grounds and river, and to be able to resume writing *Bouvard and Pécuchet*. He was now on Chapter Three, in which the two clerks try to understand chemistry and medicine and anatomy – a section on which he had done some work five years earlier as the two main characters began to take clearer shape in his mind. Writing was slow and taxing, for he needed to ridicule Bouvard and Pécuchet as emblems of stupidity, yet at the same time portray them as worthy of sympathy and respect, as their naive curiosity repeatedly leads to failure. A balance was required between the farcical and the pathetic, between irony and innocence, as he tried to show his readers the fundamental unknowability of the world and make them recognize their absurd selves in the two clerks – as he himself did. He thought of the work as a comic counterpart to *The Temptation of St Anthony*, a contemporary version of the saint's tortured, obsessive quest for ultimate enlightenment. As he sat copying from the sourcebooks that he read compulsively in preparation for writing, he identified with Bouvard and Pécuchet quite as much as with the hermit-saint. By the end, Flaubert would have consulted some 1,500 volumes for this novel, but in parts of Chapter Three he could rely on disturbing memories that still lingered from his hospital childhood. Here, however, they are tamed into comic absurdity while still retaining 'something frightening': an image of a flayed man; a midwifery tutor's leather replica of the lower half of a pregnant woman complete with removable foetus; an anatomical model by Auzoux showing veins, nerves and arteries, and with its face half-detached to reveal a monstrous dangling eyeball.[23]

Soon he settled into a satisfying daily routine, which he described in a letter to Princess Mathilde:

> My (basically austere) life is calm and peaceful on the surface. It is the life of a monk and a workman. Each day is the same – reading and more reading; my white paper becomes covered in black, and I extinguish my lamp in the middle of the night. Shortly before dinner, I swim in the river like a newt – and on it goes.[24]

In September he and Laporte returned to the Calvados area to explore the archaeology and geology of Bouvard and Pécuchet's home territory. Other friends were recruited to help in his research.

Seeking 'a cliff *that will frighten* my two fellows', he pressed Maupassant, who knew the area well, to provide a description of the entire coastline between Bruneval and Étretat, including names and descriptions of each little valley and the time it would take to walk from one to the next.[25] Laporte was quizzed about the decor of a priest's dining room ('Is there a crucifix, a religious image, a bust of the holy Father?').[26] Taine was asked about universal suffrage and the origin of the divine right of kings. And from Daudet, Flaubert borrowed a set of documents about the Duc d'Angoulême, whose life Bouvard and Pécuchet memorably fail to reconstruct.

In Paris from the end of December until the end of May 1878, Flaubert continued his obsessive programme of reading at what he claimed was an average rate of two volumes a day. His eyes hurt. Work continued on his return to Croisset, and by September, already into his sixth chapter, he could finally glimpse the end.

His confident progress was shattered, however, when he realized that Commanville's business was once again in serious trouble. 'God knows what will become of us!' he wailed, as all his financial anxieties resurfaced.[27] He no longer trusted Caroline's husband; he feared for the future; and above all, he hated being dragged into the whole sordid mess. In desperation, he even appealed to the former Gertrude Collier, now a wealthy and well-connected London widow, asking if she knew any English industrialists who might be willing to invest in Commanville's company, and enclosing a prospectus. Although Flaubert was furious about the loss of money and the restrictions it would impose on his life, worse still was the humiliation of being forced to concern himself with commercial matters: 'I feel as if my mind has been *sullied* by these base preoccupations . . . I feel I am turning into a grocer.'[28] In the hope that work might help to block out his distress, he continued to prepare notes for the eighth chapter of *Bouvard and Pécuchet*, but reading texts on metaphysics only deepened his misery.

To avoid the expense of Paris life, Flaubert was obliged to stay on in Croisset over the particularly harsh winter of 1878–9. Rain leaked through the ceiling of the old house. Stepping outside on a bitterly cold day in mid-January, he slipped on a patch of ice and fell heavily, badly damaging his ankle and fracturing a bone in his leg. To his intense displeasure the accident was reported in the press. 'I am ннннindignant! I do not like the Public knowing anything about me,' he raged to Caroline.[29] In a strange way, however, the fall seems to have revived his spirits. Laporte moved temporarily into the house to assist his bedridden friend and help reply to the many letters arriving from friends and admirers who had been alarmed by the newspaper reports. What had initially appeared to be a badly sprained ankle turned out to be a foot so severely injured that amputation seemed a possibility, but after spending eighteen days confined to bed with his leg and foot encased in an unbearably tight cast, Flaubert was able to move slowly and painfully around his room wearing a heavy but less uncomfortable splint. Fearful of entrusting his considerable weight to the crutches he had ordered, he shuffled along with his knee resting on a chair that he pushed in front of him. His doctor warned that it would be at least another month before he could go downstairs, and that he would limp for a long time to come.

Meanwhile, close friends tried to find some means of alleviating Flaubert's financial distress. He dismissed Taine's suggestion that he apply to Paris's Bibliothèque Mazarine for the post of librarian, which Taine knew was about to fall vacant, but after Turgenev made a special trip to Croisset to try to persuade his friend to change his mind, Flaubert gave in, only to discover, humiliatingly, that the position had been awarded to the incumbent's son-in-law and that his rebuff had made front-page news in *Le Figaro*. This renewed press intrusion enraged him more than ever:

I do not deserve this! Cursed be the day I ever had the
disastrous idea of putting my name to a book! If it had
not been for Bouilhet and my mother, I would never
have published! How I regret it now! I demand to be
forgotten, to be left in peace, never to be talked about![30]

He felt that *Le Figaro* had dragged him through the mud, but he
also blamed himself for having compromised his principles in
agreeing to accept paid employment: 'My life has lost all dignity.
I see myself as a soiled man.'[31] Money remained a pressing
problem, but when his friends' renewed efforts resulted in the
offer of a government pension and an honorary position at the
library involving no duties, he was initially too proud to accept.
He would not accept charity; he refused to be pitied. 'From all that
I once had, I have retained only my *pride*. Let it not be taken from
me! I would be unable to write,' he told Maupassant.[32] But when
Maupassant gave him an absolute assurance that the pension would
never become public knowledge, Flaubert gratefully relented,
surprised and touched by the official gesture from Jules Ferry, the
minister responsible, and relieved to have the modest income.

Ernest Commanville's sawmill was sold the next day, soon
followed by the sale of other Commanville property, but the
proceeds still failed to cover the full extent of Caroline's husband's
huge deficit. Flaubert could not understand why the sales allowed
some creditors to be reimbursed, while others – including himself
– received nothing. Commanville's failure to repay Laporte was
particularly distressing to Flaubert, who had persuaded his
friend to contribute a sum he could ill afford. Above all, Flaubert
felt demeaned by having to think about money, sign financial
documents he did not understand and behave like a tradesman.

Weakened by his enforced immobility and racked with anxiety
over Commanville's affairs, Flaubert sensed his health deteriorate.
Although he had been able to hobble downstairs since mid-March,

by evening his foot was always painful and swollen. Toothache, lumbago, insomnia, rheumatism, headaches, eye problems and the usual boils all added to his discomfort. His doctor prescribed valerian and more potassium bromide, but in his depressed and exhausted state, Flaubert often found himself in tears. All he could do was persevere with *Bouvard and Pécuchet*. By the beginning of June he was well enough to go to Paris for a few weeks, lodging in the Commanvilles' apartment while they moved into Croisset, and spending most afternoons in the Bibliothèque nationale taking notes on matters ecclesiastical. 'Work is the only thing that gives me pleasure now,' he told Caroline, though he again conceded that taking on such a huge and difficult project as *Bouvard and Pécuchet* had been an act of madness.[33]

Yet as his mood gradually lifted, his mind began to fill with new ideas. That September, as he packed his trunk after another Paris visit, he chatted to Edmond de Goncourt about his future plans: two more chapters of *Bouvard and Pécuchet* remained to be written, and then he would revise and organize the notes he had collected over the years and which Laporte had been helping him to classify – examples of banal, stupid or contradictory assertions copied from a vast array of writers, which were to form *Bouvard and Pécuchet*'s second volume; once that was done, there would be a volume of short stories; after that, a work following several Rouen families from before the French Revolution to the present, which he thought might take the form of a series of dialogues with detailed passages of *mise en scène*; and then he would move on to his big Second Empire novel, *Sous Napoléon III*. 'But above all,' he added,

I need . . . to rid myself of something that is obsessing me – yes, by God! – obsessing me: it's my *Battle of Thermopylae* . . . In these Greek warriors I see a troop of men devoted to death, going forward to meet it with irony and good cheer.[34]

Although Flaubert never did write about the famous battle, the honour and self-sacrifice of those ancient Greeks chimed with his own sense of fighting against overwhelming odds, sacrificing his life in the name of art, and, as always, observing himself with amused and ironic detachment.

In October 1879 he received the unexpected news that his government pension was to be doubled. This bonus, together with the income from his writing and a small allowance that his brother had promised, meant that he would have enough to live on. He was even able to entertain a fantasy of travelling to Greece with Georges Pouchet to visit Thermopylae once he had finished *Bouvard and Pécuchet*. But he wondered whether by then the novel might have killed him.

Although Flaubert knew it would take at least another year to complete both volumes, the forthcoming publication of *Bouvard and Pécuchet* was announced in the press that December. By March 1880 the final chapter of Volume One was well under way, and although he complained as usual about the laborious process of writing, he was in much better spirits now that the end was clearly in sight. Caroline sent him excellent suggestions about how to describe Pécuchet's failure to apply the rules of perspective when drawing a landscape, for she understood her uncle's aims perfectly – unlike his friend Frédéric Baudry, who was understandably baffled by a request to provide a general botanical axiom, the name of a common spring flower that was an exception to the rule, and the name of a plant that contradicted the exception. Receiving no satisfactory reply, Flaubert left an X in his manuscript to be completed later and continued writing, eager to reach the end.

At Easter he invited a group of literary friends – Daudet, Zola, Goncourt, Maupassant and Charpentier – to spend the weekend at Croisset. Keen to repay their hospitality, he laid on generous quantities of wine and had his servant Suzanne produce a special meal of turbot in cream sauce, and as the guests exchanged obscene

27. avril 1880.   SAINT POLYCARPE.

ÉDUCATION SENTIMENTALE

MADAME BOVARY   SALAMMBÔ

LA TENTATION DE ST ANTOINE

M. Gustave Flaubert.

MENU

Potage velouté à la Bovary
Saumon, sauce Mathô
Poulet Homais
Filet. Éducation Sentimentale
Jambon St Antoine
Salade au Cœur Simple
Haricots verts, Hamilcar
Glace Salammbô
Fromage (aux mangeurs de choses immondes.)
Dessert
café. Vins St Julien (Legende.). champagne sec

Menu from the St Polycarp dinner held in Flaubert's honour on 27 April 1880.

anecdotes after a raucous dinner, the house rang with Flaubert's great outbursts of laughter. There was more hilarity on 27 April, the feast day of St Polycarp, the second-century Christian martyr famous for his indignant cry of 'Oh Lord! Lord, in what times you have made me live!' Flaubert had light-heartedly adopted Polycarp as his patron saint, often using the name to sign his letters and once saying he intended to dedicate *Bouvard and Pécuchet* to the saint's memory. That year Charles Lapierre and his wife marked the day by preparing an elaborate entertainment in Flaubert's honour. The menu, decorated with an image of the saint embracing Emma Bovary and Salammbô, featured dishes named after his works. Specially composed poems were read, and he received some thirty letters and three telegrams of good wishes purporting to come from Italian cardinals, cesspool workers and his old adversary Pinard, as well as warm messages from real friends. His saint's day gifts included silk socks and a tooth presented as a relic of St Polycarp.

Ten days later Maxime Du Camp received a buoyant note from Flaubert announcing that he had almost finished *Bouvard and Pécuchet* and would shortly be coming to Paris. On the following day, 8 May 1880, a two-word telegram was delivered to Edmond de Goncourt in the capital. It read, '*Flaubert dead!*'[35]

A shocked Goncourt and other friends alerted by Maupassant's telegram congregated in Rouen for the funeral. There, they learned that Flaubert had collapsed suddenly in his study that Saturday morning, having apparently suffered a stroke – though there were also rumours that the cause of death was an epileptic fit brought on by worry about Commanville's affairs. But whatever the truth of the matter, Flaubert had died on his old Turkish divan, not consumed by a flash of lightning as he had often wished, but almost as suddenly, and without suffering.

After a simple service in the small parish church at Canteleu, the funeral cortège made its way down through the spring hedgerows to Rouen, where it was joined by people from the town.

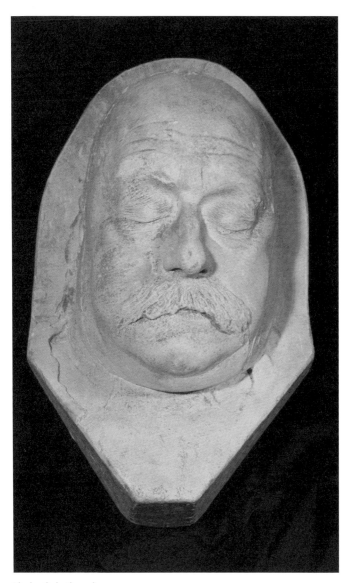

Flaubert's death mask.

Some curious bystanders, hearing the name Flaubert, assumed that the deceased must be the respected doctor Achille, while others came only to gape at the throng of Parisian journalists who had arrived to report on the death of the famous author. Then came the long, slow climb up the steep hill, past clusters of lilac and mayblossom, to the monumental cemetery with its panoramic view of the town and the curve of the river and the distant hills, where Flaubert was finally laid to rest next to his father, mother and beloved sister, and near the grave of Louis Bouilhet.

That December, three days after what would have been Flaubert's 59th birthday, the *Nouvelle revue* published the first instalment of the still unfinished *Bouvard and Pécuchet*. By then, the old house at Croisset had been sold to industrialists and demolished to make way for a distillery.

10

Flaubert's Legacy

GLORY. Is but a wisp of smoke.

Gustave Flaubert, *Dictionary of Received Ideas*

Flaubert's fame had spread far beyond France by the time of his death. Today, with his work translated into some 25 languages and continuing to sell in numbers that would have been inconceivable to him, he is universally recognized as one of the most important figures of world literature. His novels have not only been read and enjoyed by millions, but have constantly inspired, influenced and challenged writers who came after him. In the words of a recent critic, 'Flaubert changed literature forever.'[1]

Although he vehemently rejected any suggestion that he was the leader of a literary movement and insisted that art could never be reduced to a set of realist or naturalist rules, his influence was already evident during his lifetime. By 1880 he was so inundated with novels sent 'in homage' by aspiring new authors that he begged his publisher to stop forwarding them, but the adulation persisted. The group of young naturalist writers who had gathered round Zola in the 1870s hailed Flaubert as their master and referred to *Sentimental Education* as their bible, admiring especially the way Flaubert introduced believable characters into a contemporary setting, closely observed and vividly conveyed. When they presented him with a copy of *Les Soirées de Médan* (*Evenings at Médan*) dedicated to him as 'friend and master',

Copy of *Les Soirées de Médan* (Paris, 1880), dedicated to Flaubert as 'friend and master' and signed by its authors – Émile Zola, Guy de Maupassant, J.-K. Huysmans, Henry Céard, Léon Hennique and Paul Alexis.

however, the carefully researched descriptions of material reality in their collection of stories about the Franco-Prussian War left him unimpressed. For Flaubert, the documentation of detail from real life was merely a starting point, the springboard to a higher ideal. The authors of *Les Soirées de Médan* had failed to appreciate this, and their adherence to naturalist principles had resulted in work that was dull and formulaic. As an exasperated Flaubert pointed out, '*There is no such thing as truth!* There are only ways of seeing.'[2]

Although few writers could equal the mesmeric beauty and sonority of his prose, with its rhythmic cadences, its subtle, often humorous irony, its multilayered meanings and painstakingly crafted style – qualities often lost in translation – Flaubert's literary influence is now so ubiquitous as to be barely noticeable. He showed that it was possible to write great fiction about ordinary people doing ordinary things. Novelists have absorbed this lesson together with his clever placing of telling details, his use of multiple viewpoints and his innovative use of free indirect style to convey characters' unexpressed thoughts and feelings. Much admired, too, is Flaubert's cultivation of an ambiguous narrative mode that demands engagement from his readers while leaving them hovering uncertainly between several interpretations, with the result that his novels seem intriguingly different at each rereading.

Indeed, for Mario Vargas Llosa, Flaubert's greatest contribution has been to liberate readers from the idea that a novel can be read in only one way. He argues that today's novelists can learn 'everything that is essential to the modern novel' from *Madame Bovary*.[3] Although Tolstoy's *Anna Karenina* (1877) and Fontane's *Effi Briest* (1894) owe much to that novel's portrayal of an unhappily married woman, Flaubert's profound effect on subsequent literature is by no means limited to *Madame Bovary*. Moreover, just as his novels appear to evolve each time they are reread, so his influence has changed over the years as the focus shifts between different aspects of his writing. Flaubert's work moves with the times.

His discreet presence is detectable throughout the work of Marcel Proust, who was particularly sensitive to the originality of Flaubert's literary style, which he believed had 'renewed . . . our vision of things' through the entirely new way it used definite and indefinite past tenses, present participles, and certain pronouns and prepositions.[4] Proust's English contemporary Ford Madox Ford was equally aware that Flaubert had transformed the way literature was written, but he attributed Flaubert's impact to more than stylistic originality: 'What Flaubert gave to the world was not merely one book – nor five nor six; it was a whole habit of mind that is changing the face of the globe.'[5] He especially admired Flaubert's disregard for the convention of ending a novel with a marriage or a death, and for acknowledging that things carry on 'with equanimity and very little shock', as Ford put it.[6] Oscar Wilde, too, acknowledged Flaubert as his master, though for him, inspiration came mainly from the oriental works – *The Temptation of St Anthony*, *Salammbô* and *Hérodias*. Wilde considered his Salomé to be 'the sister of Salammbô', and when accused of imitating Flaubert to the point of plagiarism, he responded with characteristic panache: 'Of course I plagiarise . . . I never read Flaubert's *Tentation de saint Antoine* without signing my name at the end of it.' Eventually, he claimed, he would turn into 'Flaubert II'.[7]

Bouvard and Pécuchet proved particularly exciting to modernist writers, although when Flaubert's unfinished novel was published in 1881 it had met with bemusement or worse. Critics at the time were disconcerted by the strangeness of a work whose characters and plot seemed, in the words of one, to be 'an insult to common sense', while Barbey d'Aurevilly simply dismissed it as 'unreadable and unbearable'.[8] Yet a few decades later, many writers found the novel to be a revelation. Ezra Pound saw James Joyce's *Ulysses* (1922) as continuing a process that Flaubert had begun in *Bouvard and Pécuchet*, and he likened Joyce's writing to Flaubertian prose in English. A jotting in one of the *Finnegans*

Wake (1939) notebooks – 'Gustave Flaubert can rest having made me' – shows how fully Joyce himself acknowledged the debt.[9] Gertrude Stein was equally beholden, claiming that Flaubert's work had shown her that a literary composition need not revolve around one central idea.[10] 'Everything I have done was influenced by Flaubert,' she admitted. Others have identified *The Temptation of St Anthony* as the trigger for modernism. Michel Foucault called it 'the first literary work whose exclusive domain is that of books', arguing that after *The Temptation* 'Mallarmé is able to write *Le Livre* and modern literature is activated . . . The library is on fire.'[11]

The next generation of writers was no less admiring. Raymond Queneau wrote three prefaces for *Bouvard and Pécuchet*, a work whose puncturing of certainties so fascinated and delighted him that he ranked it as one of Western literature's greatest works alongside the *Odyssey*, the *Satyricon* and *Don Quixote* – company that would have been deeply pleasing to Flaubert. For Samuel Beckett, it was the absence of authorial explanation in *Bouvard and Pécuchet* and the perseverance of its two banal clerks in the face of recurrent failure that struck a particular chord. The bleakly comic absurdity of 'pseudo-couples' in works such as *Waiting for Godot* (1953) or *Mercier et Camier* (1970) owes much to Flaubert's paired male characters. Beckett particularly admired the fact that Flaubert's fiction recognized the unexpected and the unknowable as essential elements of human experience, and he saw him as an exemplary modern author.

The litany of major authors who proclaim Flaubert as their exemplar is long. Franz Kafka considered Flaubert a 'true blood brother',[12] William Faulkner announced that he reread *Madame Bovary* every year, and writers as varied as André Gide, Ernest Hemingway, Vladimir Nabokov, Eça de Queirós and Virginia Woolf have all acknowledged a debt to him, each finding a different form of inspiration in his work. In France in the 1960s, writers such as Nathalie Sarraute and Alain Robbe-Grillet hailed Flaubert as a precursor of the *nouveau roman*. By casting aside old conventions of character and plot in his attempts to create 'books about nothing', Flaubert had succeeded, in Sarraute's eyes, in reducing the novel to 'a pure movement that is almost like abstract art'.[13] For similar reasons, Georges Perec consciously modelled his experimental novel *Things: A Story of the Sixties* (*Les Choses*, 1965) on *Sentimental Education*, incorporating many of Flaubert's sentences into his novel and echoing the ternary rhythms of Flaubert's prose. Perec later suggested that his borrowings stemmed from a desire to *be* Flaubert.

Jean-Paul Sartre had no such wish. 'I do not like Flaubert,' he proclaimed; to him Flaubert was 'a heavy Norman chap who walks in mud and drives a horse and buggy – a ponderous, provincial character'.[14] But despite his apparent antipathy, in 1971 and 1972 Sartre published three volumes of a massive work on Flaubert, unfinished at over 2,800 pages, entitled *The Family Idiot* (*L'Idiot de la famille*). Sartre's study is neither standard biography nor literary criticism. Instead, he takes Flaubert's life as a test case that will allow him to explore the epistemological problem posed at the outset: 'What, at this point in time, can we know about a man?'[15] Although Flaubert and his early work stand at the centre of this monumental study, Sartre uses them for an experiment in methodology – their main function is to serve as a conduit for the philosopher's Marxist and psychoanalytic analysis of the society and ideology of the period.

In a very different way, Flaubert's life and the extent to which one can ever know another person are also central to Julian Barnes's novel *Flaubert's Parrot* (1984). Barnes weaves his narrator's obsessive quest to gather material for a biography of Flaubert into a brilliantly inventive work full of parody, quotation and irony. Like Sartre, Barnes uses Flaubert's life and writing to reflect on wider issues – in this case, questions about fiction, truth and uncertainty, which also concerned Flaubert – and in so doing, he reveals how fully and creatively he has absorbed Flaubert's example.

Today Flaubert's literary presence is as strong as ever. Barnes's writing continues to display the depth of his engagement with 'the novelist who promoted the absolute importance of form in the novel', while in France, Michel Houellebecq has recently been described as 'Flaubert's most-gifted great-grandson', an affiliation rivalled only by the enthusiastic declaration of Turkish Nobel Prize-winner Orhan Pamuk: '*Monsieur Flaubert, c'est moi!*'[16]

But it is not only on the literary world that Flaubert has left an enduring mark. Paul Cézanne produced a series of *Temptation of St Anthony* paintings in the 1870s and steeped himself in Flaubert's writing, declaring, 'I want to be real . . . Like Flaubert. To grasp the truth in everything . . . to become self-effacing.'[17] In turn, Flaubert has been called 'the first *cubist* writer'.[18] Sigmund Freud's explorations of the subconscious were also influenced by *The Temptation of St Anthony*, which he saw as dealing with 'the real riddles of life, all the conflicts of feelings and impulses'.[19] The drama and exoticism of *Salammbô* attracted composers almost as soon as the novel was published, and although Verdi's advertised opera never materialized and Mussorgsky's *Salammbô* opera remained unfinished, Ernest Reyer's version from 1890 met with great acclaim and has been followed by a succession of other operatic treatments, including a specially composed 'Salammbô' aria for a sequence in Orson Welles's film *Citizen Kane* (1941). Like *Salammbô*, *Madame Bovary*, *Hérodias* and *The Legend of St Julian the Hospitaller* have also enjoyed operatic adaptations. The choreographer Maurice Béjart discovered *The Temptation of St Anthony* when very young – 'it literally filled a whole part of my childhood. It was decisive for me,'[20] he reminisced – and in 1967 he transposed Flaubert's work into a brilliant performance of sound and movement. Numerous musical scores have also been created around this text. Although composers have been attracted to the works that Flaubert set in a distant and exotic past, the full range of his fiction has repeatedly been adapted for stage, television, radio or film; treatments include a silent film of *Salammbô* by the pioneering Italian film-maker Arturo Ambrosio, made as early as 1911. *Madame Bovary* has been turned into ballet, *Salammbô*'s sensuality has inspired sculptors, and despite Flaubert's emphatic refusal to allow his novels to be illustrated, countless artists, including Odilon Redon, Auguste Rodin, Alphonse Mucha and David Hockney have depicted scenes from his writings.

Flaubert's work has also been gradually transformed and absorbed into popular culture, which shows a predilection for his two eponymous heroines. Emma Bovary lives on in pop song lyrics, in *romans-photos* and in a range of 'Bovary' beauty products, while the novel's scandalous origins have frequently been exploited in publications such as a 32-page Canadian version from 1945, subtitled *The Sensational Story of an Abnormal Woman*. In 2010 *Playboy* magazine printed an extract from Lydia Davis's American translation of *Madame Bovary*, billing it on the cover as 'The Most Scandalous Novel of All Time', and thus prompting other publications to produce headlines such as 'How Madame Bovary became a Bunny Girl (at the age of 154)'.[21] *Salammbô* has undergone similar transformations, with the novel's complexity cast aside in favour of glamour and romance. A French-Italian film version from 1960 (released in English as *The Loves of Salammbô*) ends happily as Mâtho's life is spared and the lovers embrace in lingering close-up. Commercial interests have often exploited the figure of Salammbô to evoke a seductive, imaginary Orient, very different from that of Flaubert's novel. One advertiser depicts her as a Japanese geisha, and her name has been used to brand items ranging from cigarettes and cigarette papers to soap and even meat extract. And like other works by Flaubert, *Salammbô* has received extensive comic book treatment. Reimagined by Philippe Druillet as a heroic fantasy in three volumes of sci-fi graphics published between 1980 and 1986. *Salammbô* has since been developed into an interactive computer game based on

Druillet's flamboyant images, with the player adopting the role of a Spendius far removed from Flaubert's original creation.

Nowadays the name of Gustave Flaubert is familiar even to many who have never read his novels, for streets, squares, schools, hotels and cafés across the world bear it in his honour. His face has featured on postage stamps, lottery tickets, sugar lumps and a 10-euro coin, and his 190th birthday was marked by a Google Doodle. 'If your work of art is good, if it is *true*, it will leave its echo,' Flaubert told Maxime Du Camp in 1852.[22] Today, the echoes left by Flaubert's work continue to resonate long and loud, and further than he could ever have imagined.

References

All French quotations from the sources below are translated by
the author.

Introduction

1 Gustave Flaubert, *Correspondance*, ed. Jean Bruneau and Yvan Leclerc,
  5 vols (Paris, 1973–2007), vol. III, pp. 35–6. Subsequent references to
  this edition are given as 'Flaubert, *Corr.*'

1 The Early Years, 1821–40

1 Flaubert, *Corr.*, vol. III, p. 142.
2 Flaubert, *Corr.*, vol. II, p. 697.
3 Flaubert, *Corr.*, vol. I, p. 4.
4 Gustave Flaubert, *Cahier intime de 1840–1841*, in *Oeuvres complètes*,
  vol. I: *Oeuvres de jeunesse*, ed. Claudine Gothot-Mersch and Guy Sagnes
  (Paris, 2001), p. 732.
5 Flaubert, *Corr.*, vol. I, p. 8.
6 Flaubert, *Corr.*, vol. III, p. 173.
7 Ibid., p. 102.
8 Flaubert, *Corr.*, vol. II, p. 15.
9 Gustave Flaubert, *Les Mémoires d'un fou*, in *Oeuvres de jeunesse*, p. 486.
10 Gustave Flaubert, *Un parfum à sentir ou les Baladins*, in *Oeuvres de
   jeunesse*, p. 112.
11 Flaubert, *Les Mémoires d'un fou*, p. 512.
12 Flaubert, *Corr.*, vol. I, p. 22.

13 Ibid., p. 29.

14 Flaubert, *Cahier intime de 1840–1841*, p. 741.

2 Coming of Age, 1840–44

1 Gustave Flaubert, *Pyrénées-Corse*, in *Oeuvres complètes*, vol. I: *Oeuvres de jeunesse*, ed. Claudine Gothot-Mersch and Guy Sagnes (Paris, 2001), p. 660.

2 Ibid., p. 681.

3 Gustave Flaubert, *Voyage en Orient*, ed. Claudine Gothot-Mersch (Paris, 2006), p. 58.

4 Gustave Flaubert, *Cahier intime de 1840–1841*, in *Oeuvres complètes*, vol. I, pp. 741–2.

5 Flaubert, *Corr.*, vol. I, p. 83

6 Flaubert, *Corr.*, vol. V, p. 941.

7 Flaubert, *Corr.*, vol. I, p. 84.

8 Ibid., p. 94.

9 Ibid.

10 Ibid., pp. 123–4.

11 David Waller, *The Magnificent Mrs Tennant* (New Haven, CT, and London, 2009), p. 77.

12 Flaubert, *Corr.*, vol. I, p. 147.

13 Maxime Du Camp, *Souvenirs littéraires*, ed. Daniel Oster (Paris, 1994), p. 188.

14 Flaubert, *Corr.*, vol. I, p. 196.

15 Ibid., p. 195.

16 Ibid.

17 Flaubert, *Corr.*, vol. II, p. 423.

18 Flaubert, *Corr.*, vol. I, p. 203.

3 Deaths and Desires, 1844–8

1 Gustave Flaubert, *L'Éducation sentimentale* (1845), in *Oeuvres complètes*, vol. I: *Oeuvres de jeunesse*, ed. Claudine Gothot-Mersch and Guy Sagnes (Paris, 2001), p. 1074.

2 Flaubert, *Corr.*, vol. I, pp. 794–5.

3 Ibid., p. 214.

4 Ibid., p. 226.

5 Ibid, p. 249.

6 Flaubert, *Corr.*, vol. V, pp. 505–6.

7 Flaubert, *Corr.*, vol. I, p. 257.

8 Ibid., p. 261.

9 Ibid., p. 258.

10 Ibid., p. 270.

11 Ibid., p. 273.

12 Ibid., p. 274.

13 Ibid., p. 280.

14 Ibid., p. 368.

15 Ibid., p. 342.

16 Ibid., p. 448.

17 Ibid., p. 460.

18 Ibid., p. 491.

19 Ibid., p. 496.

4 The Orient, 1848–51

1 Flaubert, *Corr.*, vol. I, p. 500.

2 Ibid., p. 503.

3 Ibid.

4 Ibid., p. 538.

5 Gustave Flaubert, *Voyage en Orient*, ed. Claudine Gothot-Mersch
   (Paris, 2006), p. 93.

6 Ibid., p. 99.

7 Flaubert, *Corr.*, vol. I, p. 564.

8 Ibid., p. 602.

9 Ibid., p. 612.

10 Ibid., p. 734.

11 Ibid., p. 707.

12 Ibid., p. 741.

13 Ibid., p. 709.

14 Ibid., p. 644.

15 Ibid., p. 750.
16 Ibid., p. 610.
17 Ibid., p. 783.

5 The *Madame Bovary* Years, 1851–7

1   Flaubert, *Corr.*, vol. i, p. 781.
2   Flaubert, *Corr.*, vol. ii, p. 3.
3   Ibid., p. 728.
4   Maxime Du Camp, *Souvenirs littéraires*, ed. Daniel Oster (Paris, 1994),
     p. 314.
5   Flaubert, *Corr.*, vol. ii, p. 5.
6   Ibid., p. 6.
7   Gustave Flaubert, *Madame Bovary*, in *Oeuvres complètes*, vol. iii: *1851–62*,
     ed. Claudine Gothot-Mersch, Jeanne Bem, Yvan Leclerc, Guy Sagnes
     and Gisèle Séginger (Paris, 2013), p. 454.
8   Flaubert, *Corr.*, vol. ii, pp. 10–11.
9   Ibid., p. 865.
10 Ibid., p. 13.
11 Ibid., p. 29.
12 Charles Baudelaire, *Correspondance*, ed. Claude Pichois, 2 vols
     (Paris, 1973), vol. i, p. 188.
13 Flaubert, *Corr.*, vol. ii, p. 62.
14 Ibid., p. 65.
15 Ibid., p. 31.
16 Ibid., p. 14.
17 Ibid., p. 68.
18 Ibid., p. 104.
19 Caroline Commanville, *Souvenirs intimes*, in Gustave Flaubert,
     Correspondance (Paris, 1926), vol. i, p. xix.
20 Flaubert, *Corr.*, vol. ii, p. 434.
21 Flaubert, *Corr.*, vol. iv, p. 153.
22 Flaubert, *Corr.*, vol. ii, p. 262.
23 Ibid., p. 557.
24 Ibid., p. 572.
25 Ibid., p. 483.

26 Ibid., p. 611.
27 Ibid., p. 650.
28 Ibid., p. 658.
29 Ibid., pp. 654–5.
30 Ibid., p. 697.
31 Ibid., p. 691.

6 The *Salammbô* Years, 1857–62

1 Edmond Duranty, 'Nouvelles diverses', *Réalisme* (15 March 1857), p. 79;
   Louis de Cormenin, '*Madame Bovary* par Gustave Flaubert', *Journal du
   Loiret* (6 May 1857), n.p.
2 Alfred-Auguste Cuvillier-Fleury, 'Variétés: Revue littéraire', *Journal des
   débats* (26 May 1857), n.p.
3 Flaubert, *Corr.*, vol. II, pp. 678–9.
4 Ibid., p. 691.
5 Ibid., p. 726.
6 Ibid., p. 714.
7 Edmond and Jules de Goncourt, *Journal: Mémoires de la vie littéraire*
   (Paris, 1989), vol. I, p. 488.
8 Flaubert, *Corr.*, vol. II, pp. 784–5.
9 Ibid., p. 795.
10 Ibid., p. 810.
11 Gustave Flaubert, *Voyage en Algérie et en Tunisie*, in *Oeuvres complètes*,
   vol. III: *1851–62*, ed. Claudine Gothot-Mersch, Jeanne Bem, Yvan
   Leclerc, Guy Sagnes and Gisèle Séginger (Paris, 2013), p. 864.
12 Ibid., pp. 846, 848.
13 Ibid., pp. 873, 851.
14 Ibid., p. 856.
15 Ibid., p. 881.
16 Flaubert, *Corr.*, vol. II, p. 817.
17 Ibid., p. 837.
18 Ibid., p. 843.
19 Goncourt, *Journal*, vol. I, p. 674.
20 Flaubert, *Corr.*, vol. III, p. 41.
21 Ibid., pp. 175–7.

22 Gustave Flaubert, *Salammbô* manuscripts, Bibliothèque nationale de France, n.a.fr 23.662, fol. 202v; fol. 193.

23 Flaubert, *Corr.*, vol. III, p. 170.

24 Goncourt, *Journal*, vol. I, pp. 545–6.

25 Flaubert, *Corr.*, vol. III, p. 211.

26 Ibid., p. 250, and Flaubert, *Corr.*, vol. V, p. 984.

27 Armand de Pontmartin, 'M. Gustave Flaubert – *Salammbô*', *La Gazette de France* (21 December 1862), p. 1.

28 Léon Gautier, '*Salammbô* par M. Gustave Flaubert', *Le Monde* (5 December 1862), n.p.

29 Flaubert, *Corr.*, vol. III, p. 276.

30 Ibid., p. 317.

31 Ibid., p. 270.

32 Ibid., p. 375.

33 Ibid., p. 855.

7 The *Sentimental Education* Years, 1862–9

1 Flaubert, *Corr.*, vol. III, p. 315.

2 Ibid., p. 409.

3 Ibid., p. 323.

4 Ibid., p. 362.

5 Ibid., p. 366.

6 Ibid., p. 734.

7 Ibid., p. 411.

8 Ibid., p. 425.

9 Ibid., p. 431.

10 Ibid., p. 447.

11 Ibid., p. 449.

12 Ibid., p. 456.

13 Ibid.

14 Gustave Flaubert, *L'Éducation sentimentale*, ed. P. M. Wetherill (Paris, 1984), p. 3.

15 Flaubert, *Corr.*, vol. III, p. 563.

16 Ibid., p. 374.

17 Flaubert, *L'Éducation sentimentale*, p. 125.

18 Flaubert, *Corr.*, vol. III, p. 629.

19 Ibid, p. 725.

20 Ibid., p. 727.

21 Flaubert, *Corr.*, vol. IV, pp. 36–7.

22 Ibid., p. 45.

23 Gustave Flaubert, 'Mon pauvre Bouilhet', in *Vie et travaux du R. P. Cruchard et autres inédits*, ed. Matthieu Desportes and Yvan Leclerc (Rouen, 2005), p. 87.

24 Flaubert, *Corr.*, vol. IV, p. 112.

8 Struggles and Defeats, 1869–74

1 Flaubert, *Corr.*, vol. IV, p. 77.

2 Ibid., p. 193.

3 Ibid., p. 196.

4 Ibid., p. 211.

5 Ibid., p. 218.

6 Ibid., pp. 211, 225, 231, 232, 242.

7 Ibid., p. 243.

8 Ibid., p. 244.

9 Ibid., p. 275.

10 Ibid., pp. 329, 331.

11 Ibid., p. 341.

12 Francisque Sarcey, '*Mademoiselle Aïssé*, pièce de Louis Bouilhet', *Le Temps* (8 January 1872), n.p.

13 Flaubert, *Corr.*, vol. IV, p. 441.

14 Gustave Flaubert, 'Lettre de M. Gustave Flaubert à la municipalité de Rouen', *Le Temps* (26 January 1872), n.p.

15 Flaubert, *Corr.*, vol. IV, p. 301.

16 Ibid., p. 487.

17 Ibid., p. 501.

18 Ibid., pp. 504–5.

19 Ibid., p. 517.

20 Gustave Flaubert, *La Tentation de saint Antoine*, ed. Claudine Gothot-Mersch (Paris, 1983), p. 241.

21 Ibid., p. 237.

22 Flaubert, *Corr.*, vol. IV, p. 543.

23 Ibid., pp. 547, 554.

24 Flaubert, *Corr.*, vol. III, p. 973.

25 Flaubert, *Corr.*, vol. IV, p. 717.

26 Ibid., p. 531.

27 Saint-René Taillandier, 'G. Flaubert, *La Tentation de saint Antoine*', *Revue des deux mondes* (1 May 1874), p. 223.

28 Flaubert, *Corr.*, vol. IV, p. 794.

29 Ibid., p. 793.

30 Ibid., p. 797.

31 Ibid., p. 794.

32 Ibid., pp. 818–19.

9 The Final Years, 1874–80

1 Flaubert, *Corr.*, vol. IV, p. 846.

2 Ibid., p. 559.

3 Ibid., p. 847.

4 Ibid., p. 816.

5 Ibid., p. 928.

6 Ibid., p. 942.

7 Ibid., p. 952.

8 Ibid., p. 976.

9 Ibid., p. 1001.

10 Gustave Flaubert, *Trois contes*, ed. P. M. Wetherill (Paris, 1988), p. 219.

11 Flaubert, *Corr.*, vol. V, p. 26.

12 Flaubert, *Corr.*, vol. IV, p. 1001.

13 Flaubert, *Corr.*, vol. V, p. 56.

14 Ibid., p. 64.

15 Ibid., pp. 56–7.

16 Ibid., p. 90.

17 Ibid., p. 58.

18 Ibid., pp. 180–81.

19 Flaubert, *Corr.*, vol. IV, p. 835.

20 Gustave Flaubert, *Carnets de travail*, ed. Pierre-Marc de Biasi (Paris, 1988), p. 549.

21 Flaubert, *Corr.*, vol. v, p. 195.

22 Ibid., p. 235.

23 Gustave Flaubert, *Bouvard et Pécuchet*, ed. Claudine Gothot-Mersch (Paris, 1979), p. 120.

24 Flaubert, *Corr.*, vol. v, p. 267.

25 Ibid., p. 314.

26 Ibid., p. 341.

27 Ibid., p. 472.

28 Ibid., p. 473.

29 Ibid., p. 512.

30 Ibid., p. 554.

31 Ibid.

32 Ibid., p. 571.

33 Ibid., p. 657.

34 Edmond and Jules Goncourt, *Journal: Mémoires de la vie littéraire* (Paris, 1989), vol. ii, pp. 842–3.

35 Ibid., p. 862.

10 Flaubert's Legacy

1 James Wood, 'How Flaubert Changed Literature Forever', *New Republic* (12 December 2014), www.newrepublic.com, accessed 28 March 2017.

2 Flaubert, *Corr.*, vol. v, p. 811.

3 Mario Vargas Llosa, 'Flaubert, Our Contemporary', in *The Cambridge Companion to Flaubert*, ed. Timothy Unwin (Cambridge, 2004), p. 220.

4 Marcel Proust, 'A propos du "style" de Flaubert', *Nouvelle Revue Française*, 76 (January 1920), p. 72.

5 Ford Maddox Ford, *Thus to Revisit* (London, 1921), pp. 160–61.

6 Ford Maddox Ford, *The English Novel* (London, 1930), p. 126.

7 Richard Ellmann, *Oscar Wilde* (London, 1987), p. 376.

8 Auguste Sabatier, 'Variétés: L'Oeuvre posthume de G. Flaubert', *Journal de Genève* (3 April 1881), n.p.; Barbey d'Aurevilly, '*Bouvard et Pécuchet* par Gustave Flaubert', *Le Constitutionnel* (20 May 1882), n.p.

9 James Joyce, *The Finnegans Wake Notebooks at Buffalo*, ed. Vincent Deane, Daniel Ferrer and Geert Lernout (Turnhout, 2001–2), vib/8, p. 71.

10 Gertrude Stein, 'A Transatlantic Interview', quoted in Michael J. Hoffman, *Gertrude Stein* (Boston, MA, 1976), p. 140.

11 Michel Foucault, 'Fantasia of the Library', in *Language, Counter-memory, Practice: Selected Essays and Interviews*, ed. Donald F. Bouchard, trans. Donald F. Bouchard and Sherry Simon (Ithaca, NY, 1977), p. 92.

12 Franz Kafka, *Briefe an Felice*, ed. E. Heller and J. Born (Frankfurt, 1967), p. 460.

13 Nathalie Sarraute, *Paul Valéry et l'Enfant d'Éléphant, suivi de Flaubert le précurseur* (Paris, 1986), p. 89.

14 'Entretien avec Jean-Paul Sartre' (Sartre interviewed by Catherine Clément and Bernard Pingaud), *L'Arc*, 79, *Gustave Flaubert* (1980), p. 33.

15 Jean-Paul Sartre, *The Family Idiot: Gustave Flaubert 1821–1857*, trans. Carol Cosman (Chicago, IL, and London, 1981), vol. I, p. ix.

16 'Hay Festival Cartagena: Julian Barnes and Mario Vargas Llosa talk about Flaubert', *The Telegraph* (8 February 2013), www.telegraph.co.uk, accessed 28 March 2017; Dominique Noguez, *Houellebecq en fait* (Paris, 2003), p. 74; Orhan Pamuk, 'Monsieur Flaubert, c'est moi!', lecture given at University of Rouen, 17 March 2009, text available at http://flaubert. univ-rouen.fr/etudes/pamuk_anglais.php, accessed 28 March 2017.

17 Michael Doran, ed., *Conversations with Cézanne*, trans. J. L. Cochran (London, 2001), p. 154.

18 Gérard Genette, 'Flaubert par Proust', *L'Arc*, 79, *Gustave Flaubert* (1980), p. 17.

19 Quoted in Ernest Jones, *The Life and Work of Sigmund Freud: The Formative Years and the Great Discoveries, 1856–1900* (London, 1953), p. 175.

20 'Béjart parle de Flaubert' (Bejart interviewed by Christian Descamps), *L'Arc*, 79, *Gustave Flaubert* (1980), p. 44.

21 John Lichfield, 'How Madame Bovary Became a Bunny Girl (at the Age of 154)', *Independent* (3 September 2010), www.independent.co.uk, accessed 28 March 2017.

22 Flaubert, *Corr.*, vol. II, p. 114.

Select Bibliography

Works by Flaubert

Carnets de travail, ed. Pierre-Marc de Biasi (Paris, 1988)
Correspondance, ed. Jean Bruneau and Yvan Leclerc, 5 vols
  (Paris, 1973–2007)
Oeuvres complètes, vol. I: *Oeuvres de jeunesse*, ed. Claudine Gothot-Mersch
  and Guy Sagnes (Paris, 2001)
Oeuvres complètes, vol. II: *1845–51*, ed. Claudine Gothot-Mersch,
  Stéphanie Dord-Crouslé, Yvan Leclerc, Guy Sagnes and Gisèle
  Séginger (Paris, 2013)
Oeuvres complètes, vol. III: *1851–62*, ed. Claudine Gothot-Mersch, Jeanne
  Bem, Yvan Leclerc, Guy Sagnes and Gisèle Séginger (Paris, 2013)
Vie et travaux du R. P. Cruchard et autres inédits, ed. Matthieu Desportes
  and Yvan Leclerc (Rouen, 2005)

Works by Flaubert in English translation

Bouvard and Pecuchet, with the Dictionary of Received Ideas, trans.
  A. J. Krailsheimer (London, 1976)
Early Writings, trans. Robert Griffin (Lincoln, NE, and London, 1991)
The Letters of Gustave Flaubert, 1830–1857, selected, ed. and trans.
  Francis Steegmuller (London, 1981)
The Letters of Gustave Flaubert, 1857–1880, selected, ed. and trans.
  Francis Steegmuller (London, 1984)
Madame Bovary, trans. Geoffrey Wall (London, 2003)
Mémoires d'un fou/Memoirs of a Madman, trans. Timothy Unwin
  (Liverpool, 2001)

November, trans. Frank Jellinek (London, 1966)

Salammbô, trans. A. J. Krailsheimer (London, 1977)

Selected Letters, ed. and trans. Geoffrey Wall (London, 1997)

Sentimental Education, trans. Robert Baldick and Geoffrey Wall
        (London, 2004)

The Temptation of St Anthony, trans. Lafcadio Hearn (London, 1983)

Three Tales, trans. Roger Whitehouse (London, 2005)

Critical works on Flaubert in English

Addison, Claire, *Where Flaubert Lies: Chronology, Mythology and History*
        (Cambridge, 1996)

Bloom, Harold, ed., *Gustave Flaubert* (New York and Philadelphia, PA, 1988)

Brombert, Victor, *The Novels of Flaubert: A Study of Themes and Techniques*
        (Princeton, NJ, 1966)

Culler, Jonathan, *Flaubert: The Uses of Uncertainty* (London and Ithaca,
        NY, 1974)

Donatio, Eugenio, *The Script of Decadence: Essays on the Fictions of Flaubert
        and the Poetics of Romanticism* (Oxford and New York, 1993)

Fairlie, Alison, *Flaubert: 'Madame Bovary'* (London, 1962)

Gans, Eric, *The Discovery of Illusion: Flaubert's Early Works, 1835–1837*
        (Berkeley, CA, 1971)

Green, Anne, *Flaubert and the Historical Novel: 'Salammbô' Reassessed*
        (Cambridge, 1982)

Green, Anne, Mary Orr and Timothy Unwin, eds, *Flaubert: Shifting
        Perspectives*, Dix-Neuf, XV/1 (April 2011)

Haig, Stirling, *Flaubert and the Gift of Speech: Dialogue and Discourse in Four
        'Modern' Novels* (Cambridge, 1986)

Heath, Stephen, *Flaubert: 'Madame Bovary'* (Cambridge, 1992)

Israel-Pelletier, Aimée, *Flaubert's Straight and Suspect Saints: The Unity of
        'Trois Contes'* (Amsterdam and Philadelphia, PA, 1991)

Knight, Diana, *Flaubert's Characters: The Language of Illusion*
        (Cambridge, 1985)

Lloyd, Rosemary, *Flaubert: 'Madame Bovary'* (London, 1989)

Neiland, Mary, *'Les Tentations de saint Antoine' and Flaubert's Fiction:
        A Creative Dynamic* (Amsterdam, 2001)

Orr, Mary, *Flaubert: Writing the Masculine* (Oxford, 2000)

Porter, Laurence M., ed., *Critical Essays on Gustave Flaubert* (Boston, MA, 1986)

—, ed., *A Gustave Flaubert Encyclopedia* (Westport, CT, 2001)

Raitt, Alan, *Flaubert's First Novel: A Study of the 1845 'Éducation sentimentale'* (Bern, 2010)

—, *Flaubert: 'Trois contes'* (London, 1991)

Rees, Kate, *Flaubert: Transportation, Progression, Progress* (Oxford, 2010)

Sartre, Jean-Paul, *The Family Idiot, Gustave Flaubert, 1821–1857*, trans. Carol Cosman, 5 vols (Chicago, IL, and London, 1981–93)

Tooke, Adrianne, *Flaubert and the Pictorial Arts: From Image to Text* (Oxford, 2000)

Unwin, Timothy, ed., *The Cambridge Companion to Flaubert* (Cambridge, 2004)

Vargas Llosa, Mario, *The Perpetual Orgy: Flaubert and 'Madame Bovary'* (London and Boston, MA, 1987)

Williams, D. A., *'The Hidden Life at its Source': A Study of Flaubert's 'L'Éducation sentimentale'* (Hull, 1987)

—, and Mary Orr, eds, *New Approaches in Flaubert Studies* (Lewiston, NY, 1999)

Online resources on Flaubert

Centre Flaubert (University of Rouen): http://flaubert.univ-rouen.fr

Acknowledgements

I am very grateful to the French department of King's College London for their contribution towards the cost of this book's images, as for much else. I am also indebted to the University of Rouen's Centre Flaubert, whose excellent website is an invaluable resource for all Flaubert specialists, and to the Musée Flaubert et d'histoire de la médecine in Rouen for permission to photograph some of the exhibits. I should also like to thank all those friends and colleagues who have helped with information, advice and encouragement, particularly Yvan Leclerc, Robert Lethbridge, Heather Glen, Jo Malt, Francesco Manzini and Bénédicte Percheron. Vivian Constantinopoulos and her colleagues at Reaktion have overseen the production of this book with exemplary goodwill and expertise, and to them, too, I owe a real debt of gratitude.

Photo Acknowledgements

The author and publishers wish to express their thanks to the below sources of illustrative material and/or permission to reproduce it.

Bibliothèque municipale de Rouen: pp. 16, 18, 26, 84, 97, 144; published by Carjat et Cie: pp. 6, 102; photo by Anne Green: p. 152; Musée Comtois, Ville de Besançon: p. 47; Musée Flaubert et d'histoire de la médecine, Rouen (photos by Anne Green): pp. 10, 12, 14, 21, 39, 49, 137, 150: Musée Granet, Aix-en-Provence: p. 55; Musée de l'Histoire de France, Château de Versailles: p. 91; published in *L'Illustrateur des dames* (22 February 1863): p. 107; published in *Mémoires de l'academie royale de médecine* (Paris, 1838), vol. VII: p. 81; published in *La Parodie* (5–12 December 1869): p. 89; © Photothèque Musée Picasso, Antibes: p. 20; private collection: p. 166; Roger-Viollet/Rex Features/Shutterstock: pp. 121, 163; Service Archives et Documentation de la Ville de Rouen 215/109: p. 29; published by Witz et Cie, Rouen: p. 112.